What Readers Are Saying ...

"For a book to expand the reader's perspective, the words must come from a place of thoughtful, meditative experience. For the contents to touch the heart, they must come from the inner depths of the author's life. When a compelling invitation to change occurs, it's when the composer is living from the score they have created. Peggy Adams's book does all this and more as she has mastered the art of writing what she lives in *Journey in the Secret Place.* What a delightful journal on how you, too, can have an intimate walk with Jesus!"

~ Dr. James W. Goll
Founder, God Encounters Ministries & Global Prayer Storm,
Author, Instructor, Advisor, Singer, and TV Host

"Peggy has beautifully crafted her own personal journey with her Bridegroom King, Jesus Christ. I was captivated and drawn to her journey as it had the essence of a personal invitation to find the same place of wonder and delight in the King that she found. As a personal friend for several years, I can wholeheartedly endorse her journey as she is a woman of substance, truth, and integrity. I pray you sense the heart of the Lord calling you into the depths of His heart as well. Begin your own journey! Thank you, Peggy, for your bold display of a surrendered life, highlighted in these pages!"

~ Ruth Mangiacapre
Impact Ministry, USA Director, Women on the Front Lines

"Among my favorite things to do is to see and experience Jesus in someone else's story. By story, I mean their life journey. *Journey in the Secret Place* by my good friend, Peggy Adams, is a special portion of her authentic and intimate journey with Jesus. It impacted me deeply for several reasons. First, because I know Peggy, I felt like I was there with her. In other words, knowing her personally made it so much more real for me. Second, my personal hunger for Jesus was awakened and nourished over and over again. Third, God's heart for His children jumped off every page. Whether you know Peggy or not, you may be sure that her story is full of Jesus, for your story. Always remember: what the Holy Spirit does for one of us is with all of us in mind. You are part of the story! *You* are in this book!"

~ **Dr. Bill Bennot**
Church Planter, Pastor, Author, Strategic Leader

"From the very first page of *Journey in the Secret Place*, Peggy Adams ushers readers into the tender presence of the Lord with authenticity, humility, and a contagious passion for intimacy with Jesus. Her story is not simply a testimony. I believe it is an intentional invitation. Through her forty-day journey of consecration and communion with her Beloved King, Peggy offers a transparent window into what it means to dwell under the shadow of the Almighty and to be transformed by His love.

Having served alongside Peggy in intercessory ministry through the Nashville House of Prayer, King's Hill House of Prayer, and Pray Nashville, I have witnessed firsthand her unwavering devotion to the Secret Place, seeking the heart of God in prayer, worship, and stillness before Him for countless hours, days, weeks, and even months. This book carries the fragrance of those encounters. It is saturated with the presence of the Lord and will inspire believers everywhere to quiet their hearts, return to their First Love, and embrace a lifestyle of abiding intimacy with Jesus."

~**Barbara Ann Jeter,**
Board Chair, King's Hill House of Prayer & Eternal Heiress Ministries

"For as long as I've known her, my dear friend and prayer partner, Peggy Adams, has hungered for a deeper intimacy with Jesus. This amazing book, *Journey in the Secret Place*, beautifully chronicles Peggy's spiritual journey as one who has chosen to live a lifestyle from Psalm 91:1, "He who dwells in the secret place of the Most High shall abide under the shadow of the Almighty." Peggy weaves personal stories with biblical insights, inviting readers to find comfort, strength, and encouragement in their faith.

This book is not only informative and inspirational but also practical. It offers a roadmap for those desiring spiritual renewal and growth in their relationship with the Lord. I highly recommend this anointed book as a must-read for anyone seeking a deeper understanding of their own personal journey with Jesus."

~ Dr Bob Perry
Founder, Workplace Prayer,
Pastor, Intercessor, Coach, Author and Missionary

"*Journey in the Secret Place* is a beautiful invitation into the heart of a woman who refuses to settle for anything less than the fullness of God. With every page, Peggy S. Adams draws you deeper into her intimate pursuit of the One she calls Beloved. As I read, my own heart ached with longing—longing for more of His presence, more of His nearness, more of the tender whispers she so vulnerably shares.

Peggy doesn't just tell a story; she opens a doorway. She leads us through her personal journey of hunger, surrender, and devotion, and in doing so, she stirs the same holy desire within us. This book is a gift for anyone desperate to experience all that God has for them. It will awaken your spirit, soften your heart, and call you deeper into the secret place where transformation begins."

~Missy Maxwell Worton
Award-Winning Author of *Don't Mess With This Mama*
CEO & founder of Warrior Writers Training & Light Warrior Publishing

"Peggy Adams is an Overcomer. She has learned to respond consistently to the invitation of her King in going deeper and deeper into intimacy with Him despite obstacles, impediments and resistance. This book is written from a place of integrity birthed through her authentic *Journey in the Secret Place.* Even with thirty years of my journey behind me and more to come, I am discovering my current need for the partnership that Peggy's writing provides. This book is helping me "return to my First Love" that can so easily move from center. We need leaders like Peggy who can show us how to prioritize the Presence and invest the time and focus to explore our inheritance in Christ. I encourage you to read these pages, take the next steps, and discover more fully your path and the inheritance prepared for you on the Journey—to go deeper, wider and higher with Him!"

~ Matthew Fleming
Marketplace Strategic Intelligence & Prayer
Omega Provision

Journey

IN THE
SECRET PLACE

Pursuing a Lifestyle of Intimacy
with the Lord

PEGGY S. ADAMS

Journey in the Secret Place

© 2025 Peggy S. Adams

Paperback ISBN: 978-1-969202-20-9
Hardback ISBN: 978-1-969202-21-6
E-book ISBN: 978-1-969202-22-3

Cover Design: Todd Engel
Editor: Anne Severance

Unless otherwise noted, all Scripture quotations are taken from the
New King James Version* (NKJV*). Copyright © 1982 by
Thomas Nelson Publishers. Used by permission. All rights reserved;
Scriptures identified as TPT are taken from The Passion Translation.
Copyright © 2017, 2018, 2020by Passion & Fire Ministries, Inc.
Used by permission. All rights reserved.

Amplified Bible (AMP). Copyright © 2015 by The Lockman Foundation.
La Habra, CA 90631. All rights reserved. The Living Bible (TLB). Copyright
© 1971 by Tyndale House Foundation. Used by permission of Tyndale House
Publishers, Inc., Carol Stream, Illinois 60188. All rights reserved.
Holy Bible, New Living Translation (NLT). Copyright © 1996, 2004,2015
by Tyndale House Foundation. Used by permission of Tyndale House
Publishers, Inc., Carol Stream, Illinois 60188. All rights reserved.

Light WARRIOR
PUBLISHING
TM

Printed in the United States of America
First Edition 2025

Dedication

First, I would like to dedicate this book to my Lord and Savior, Jesus Christ, my Bridegroom King. He not only chose me to take this journey with Him, but He patiently loved me each step of the way. I am honored to be His scribe for our book together. And I want to honor and thank Father God and Holy Spirit for being a Father and Comforter in the times when I needed them most.

I further dedicate this book to my son, Devin Adams, who is in heaven. It was his encouragement, right before his Homegoing, that convinced me that I could do this. In the moments when I couldn't write, I could hear him speak to my heart: *"Come on, Mama, you've got this!"* I know you are cheering me on from heaven, son.

"He who dwells in the secret place
of the Most High
Shall abide under the shadow
of the Almighty."

~Psalm 91:1

Contents

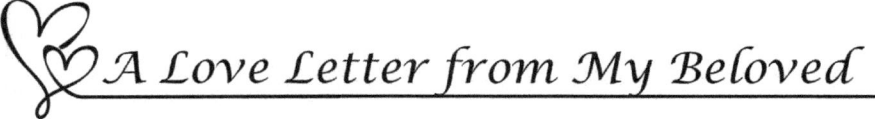

A Love Letter from My Beloved

Wave upon wave upon wave!
My sound and My song flow over you, to you,
and out of you.
No height nor depth of understanding can
comprehend My thoughts and My love for you.
You say to Me: "Lord, You are my hiding place."
But I say to you, "Peggy, you are My hiding place."
I love it when you seek Me, for during those times
when You seek Me, My ways and My heart
are revealed to you.
Walk with Me in the cool, refreshing part of the day.
Lean on Me in your times of need.
I long to be near you.
I long to encourage you, and I long to be
your Everything.
Come away, come away, My lover and My bride.
I long to take you into the secret place of My heart.
My heart desires to be one with you.
My heart desires to know the passions of your heart.
So come away, come away with Me.
My lover and My friend.

~Jesus, Your Bridegroom King

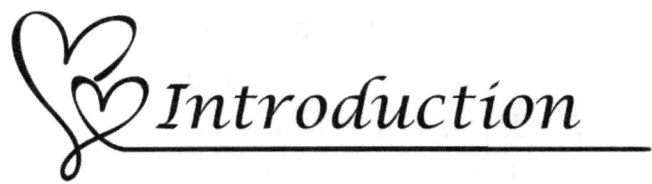# *Introduction*

For as long as I can remember, I have been a lover of books. Having grown up on a farm in a rural area of North Carolina, my two favorite things to do in my spare time were exploring in the woods, looking for creeks, and reading. I would take a book with me and sit for hours, listening to the sound of the water flowing over the rocks as I found myself immersed in a good story. At these times, I would travel, in my imagination, to faraway lands—places I'd never visited before.

In all the journeys I'd taken through books over the years, little did I know that God was preparing me for my own personal journey with Him. This would be one that would not only change my life but might help to change the lives of many others as well.

It all began with a clear call from my Beloved King Jesus, inviting me to join Him in what is referred to in Psalm 91:1 as the "secret place." Hidden away in a remote area, I spent forty days with very little contact with other people, learning more about spiritual intimacy than I would have ever known apart from His summons to come away with Him.

It was during my intimate experiences with Jesus that He taught me how to hear His voice more clearly, to sit with Him and listen in quietness, to go to greater depths of studying His Word, to learn to rest in Him and His promises, and to follow Him in obedience and trust even when I didn't understand. Above all, He taught me how to receive—and give—His boundless love.

I was so filled with fresh insights, revelation, and encounters with our King that He asked me to share them with you through this book!

The journey you are about to embark on with me is based on Isaiah 30:15:

"Thus says the Lord God, the Holy One of Israel:
*In **returning [repentance]** and **rest** you shall be saved;*
*In **quietness** and **confidence [trust]** shall be your strength."*

Some of the chapters explore the four concepts in bold type above—***returning (repentance), rest, quietness, and confidence (trust).*** These are key components in pursuing a lifestyle of intimacy with Christ, or as I often refer to Him in this book, "my Beloved or my Bridegroom King" (see *Song of Solomon)*. These titles alone draw us deeper into His heart.

You will experience moments when I bring you with me into my encounters with the Lord. At other times, we will simply reflect on what has already occurred or what is continuing to occur. It's at these times that I will teach from what is taking place and share lessons I've learned from my Beloved.

On each of the first thirty days of this journey, He gives me a specific word, Scripture, and often a song to study, to journal, and to meditate on. These are given to teach, strengthen, and encourage me, and to help me with struggles I am dealing with.

As an intercessor, it is the most natural thing for me to have a conversation with the Lord about any situation, challenge, need, or person whom He allows to cross my path. Therefore, you will find many prayers from my journal throughout this book—in no specific order. I also extend an invitation, when appropriate, for you to pray along with me. I'm a firm believer that we are all welcome to approach the throne of God with our petitions at any time and in any place. And we are asked to come **boldly!**

There are those of you who will read this book and receive fresh insight and revelation. You will be stirred with greater hunger to experience and know Jesus and the Father more deeply than ever before. Others will be reminded of things you already know, especially the price we pay and what we gain when we completely surrender ourselves to our Beloved King Jesus. I believe this book is a gift from God to everyone who reads it with a heart to know Him.

It is my hope that you will be encouraged as you use what Holy Spirit has taught me to help you overcome any challenges you may be facing. My prayer is that, through the pages of this book, you will be inspired to pursue a deeper, more intimate relationship with Jesus, so that when you do, others will see that the journey begins—and continues for a lifetime—in the secret place.

CHAPTER 1
The Call

"Call to Me, and I will answer you,
and show you great and mighty things,
which you do not know."

~Jeremiah 33:3

What a wild and crazy year 2020 turned out to be, a year that began with such promise and excitement. There was the transition from one decade to another. Hope for all the tomorrows. Expectations of a New Beginnings Year for me. I had received my ordination as a minister on September 1, 2019. This had been a dream and goal of mine after completing the School of Ministry from my church in High Point, North Carolina, on May 15, 2015. Upon receiving my ordination, I was trusting God for more opportunities to travel and speak in order to share the message of Jesus in this new year.

However, 2020 did not go in the direction that I or anyone else had anticipated. In March, the COVID-19 virus broke out, paralyzing the whole world. Fear and chaos erupted globally. With everything shut down and everyone confined to their homes, our way of life changed drastically.

Even our former ways of doing church and ministry were affected. We went from public gatherings in church buildings to Zoom and Facebook Live on computer or cell phones. Meetings were held in individual homes. With the world shut down and fear on the rampage, an explosion of prayer began to take place via conference calls throughout the day, every day. This became a huge ministry assignment for me and many other *intercessors*—"those who intervene, petition, or plead with God through prayer on behalf of another."

One topic of universal prayer in this chaotic time was the call for God's people to turn our hearts to Him. If we who belong to Him would humble ourselves, seek His face, pray, and turn from our ungodly ways, He promised to hear from heaven, forgive us, and heal our land (see 2 Chronicles 7:14).

Amid all the changes, laced with fear and confusion, God was shifting many of His people out of the old wineskin of doing ministry and into the new one He was calling them to embrace. I was one of those people.

*"And no one puts new wine into old wineskins;
or else the new wine bursts the wineskins, the
wine is spilled, and the wineskins are ruined.
But new wine must be put into new wineskins."*
~Mark 2:22

Hearing the Voice of God

In the fall of 2020, I knew the Lord was bringing about some changes in my own life. I could sense an uncomfortable feeling inside. No matter what I did, I couldn't find peace. I wasn't satisfied with the things that had once brought me joy and fulfillment. I could tell God was doing something deep within me so that He could move me out of my safe place of comfort. In fact, I was definitely *un*comfortable—almost agitated at times. And for no specific reason.

By October, I was utterly miserable. It seemed as if everything I did was from a place of duty and not beauty. I didn't even enjoy praying anymore. When I inquired of the Lord about this, I felt in my spirit that I should pull away from my prayer assignments to take a couple of weeks to seek His heart.

During this time, I knew He was calling me to let go of all that I was familiar with. While I was resisting what I knew He was asking of me, I clearly heard Him say, *"I am pulling you out of prayer!"*

"What do You mean?" I asked, still hoping I had not heard correctly. Waiting for a response but hearing nothing, I

3

dared to try once more. "Can we at least wait until after the elections?"

Surely, He would not recall a dedicated intercessor from the front lines during a major presidential election year! Again, silence, so I waited ....

God is always speaking, but often we do not take the time to listen. When I said a few paragraphs back that I had heard the Lord say, *"I am pulling you out of prayer,"* I did not hear this with my natural ears. It was more like an impression in my thoughts or hearing with my spiritual ears. Since I will be dialoguing with the Lord quite a bit throughout this journey, I wanted to share some of the different ways we hear Him speak.

The best way to hear God is through His written Word, the Bible. As we read and meditate on the Scriptures, Holy Spirit will speak to us in the areas of our life where His direction is needed.

Another way we hear Him is through our spiritual ears. When we hear this way, it's as if the words come immediately in our innermost being or in our heart. We also hear Him in our minds when the thoughts come so quickly—as if out of nowhere—so that we know they are not our own thoughts or imagination.

He may even speak audibly. In both the Old and New Testaments, God occasionally spoke in an audible voice to His people. For example, He communicated directly to such biblical characters as Abraham, Moses, David, Peter, James, John, Paul, and of course, Jesus. Today, most people go their entire lives without hearing the audible voice of God—although there are those who do!

He speaks to us through the eyes of our spirit. This can be the flash of a picture or image, a vision, or a dream. He also speaks through what we see with our natural eyes. He has spoken to me quite often in the beauty of nature, on billboard signs, and even from vehicle tags! He speaks through our other senses as well—smell, taste, touch. He speaks through numbers, the sounds of musical instruments, the lyrics to songs, and through other people.

God speaks through our perceiving or knowing—as if you know something without being told. Some may refer to this as a "gut feeling."

These are just some of the ways God communicates with His people. Once we get used to a specific language He has been using, though, He may shift to an entirely different method of communication. Our responsibility is to pay attention and listen. This causes us to draw closer to Him, which He loves. For a deeper understanding of the voice of God, I recommend the book *Hearing God's Voice Today* by James W. Goll.

A few weeks passed, and in late November, I was invited to stay with my friend Jett at her beautiful home in Fort Myers, Florida, for a couple of weeks. It was in this place of rest and quietness that I was able to press in and receive clarity on what my heavenly Father was asking of me. Beginning in January, 2021, I was to lay aside everything I was doing for a season to hide away with Jesus. Even though I had no idea what to expect, I submitted to what I knew He was calling me to do.

On my drive back from Fort Myers to my home in Nashville, I began to feel the presence of my Beloved King flood my heart as I praised, worshipped, and thanked Him for His faithfulness to me. It was in this intimate place with Him that I received more insight regarding my time away in January. He gave me specific directions on my location: Due West, South Carolina. He gave me the number of days I would be away: 40. And He even assured me that He would bless me with the necessary finances to cover all expenses.

Once again, I heard Him say, *"I'm pulling you out of prayer…"* but this time there was an additional phrase: *"**as you know it!"***

I thought about those last four words for a few seconds. So, that was it! By going away to be with Him, there would be a life-altering change in how I would view prayer and even how I would pray. I couldn't wait to hear more!

Preparation Time

On December 27, I returned to Nashville after spending a few days with my family in North Carolina for the Christmas holiday. During this time, I found myself daydreaming about what it was going to be like to be shut away from the outside world. I had moments of great anticipation along with moments of fear of the unknown.

For all my apprehension, though, I felt assured by my Beloved that it was natural to feel this way. Anytime we are called into something unfamiliar or unknown, our faith will be tested. That's part of the journey of learning to walk by faith and not by sight. If we could see all the way from beginning to end, it wouldn't be faith, and there wouldn't be spiritual growth. No matter what it felt like to me, I knew in my heart that my Beloved King was with me and that He would not ask me to step into something if He didn't believe I was ready for it.

So, for the next few days, I prepared for my time away, making sure all my responsibilities were covered. I caught up on my administrative duties and scheduled intercessors to lead the prayer calls on the days I would be gone. I felt like an expectant mother getting ready for a new baby!

JOURNEY IN THE SECRET PLACE

New Year's Eve, 2020

As I prepared to close out the old year and step into the new, I was anticipating amazing God-encounters and adventures! In my prayer time with Jesus, I heard Him say, *"While others are entering 2021 with a **war** and a **roar,** you are going in as a Bride to **consummate** and **consecrate** yourself fully to Me."*

Oh, how beautiful! I thought, smiling as I pondered those words, not fully understanding what they meant. I knew only that I was being called to a totally set-apart lifestyle of oneness with my Bridegroom King. *You lead me, my Bridegroom. I am Yours.*

You, too, may be asking, "What does He mean by the words *war* and *roar*? Or by *consummate* and *consecrate?"* The first two are not difficult to define. Having experienced my share of spiritual warfare as an intercessor, I knew that in moving into the chaotic presidential year of 2021, there would be many of us who would wage war against spiritual darkness through prayer and intercession. We would roar with the voice of authority to bring destruction to the plans of our spiritual enemies.

As I studied the words *consummate* and *consecrate,* I realized that this is part of the process of the Bride and Bridegroom coming together as one. In marriage, before consummation—"the perfect completion of the marital relationship, spiritual as well as physical intimacy"—there should be consecration to one another. To *consecrate* is "to

8

make or declare sacred; to set apart; to dedicate formally to a divine purpose."

Of course, consummation with our heavenly Bridegroom, Jesus, is different. Our consummation (intimacy) with Him is not physical but a spiritual coming together as one in our hearts. It's His presence and His Word that touch and awaken the deep places in our hearts to bring healing and restoration, refreshment, and renewal to our souls. If we are to experience a lifestyle of heart-to-heart intimacy with our King, there are times when we must consecrate ourselves afresh to Him.

"Fasten me upon your heart as a seal of fire forevermore. This living, consuming flame will seal you as My prisoner of love. My passion is stronger than the chains of death, and the grave, all-consuming as the very flashes of fire from the burning heart of God. Place this fierce, unrelenting fire over your entire being."
—Song of Songs 8:6, TPT

From My Journal

As I was preparing to close out this year, I was looking back at a writing from a daily devotional sent to me on December 31, 2015. At the time, I didn't fully understand what it meant because I was just launching out into a new season of trusting God for everything. Now, several years later, I am weeping because, without realizing it, I have been walking out this word by faith.

I leave you with this beautiful word from the Lord. I pray it ministers to you as you read it:

> *"The LORD your God carried you, as a man carries his son [or daughter], in all the way that you went, until you came to this place."*
>
> *"I bore you on eagle's wings and brought you to Myself. In My love and in My pity, I redeemed you, and I bore you and carried you all the days of old. As an eagle stirs up its nest, hovers over its young, spreading out its wings, taking them up, carrying them on its wings, so the LORD alone led [you]."*
>
> *"Even in your old age, I am He, and even to gray hairs, I will carry you. I have made you and I will bear you and I will carry you and I will deliver you. This is God, your God forever and ever. I will be your guide even to death."*
>
> *"Cast your burden on the Lord and He shall sustain you. Do not worry about your life, what you will eat or what you will drink, nor about your body, what you will put on. For your heavenly Father knows that you need all these things."*
>
> *"Thus far the Lord has led me."*
>
> ~Psalm 55:22a; Matthew 6:31 & 32b

CHAPTER 2
My Journey Begins

"Listen carefully, I am about to do a new thing,
Now it will spring forth;
Will you not be aware of it?
I will even put a road in the wilderness,
Rivers in the desert."

~Isaiah 43:19, AMP

Today was the Big Day! I was beginning to feel a little anxious. I had so many thoughts racing through my head. *Is this really happening? Am I actually going to do this? Have I lost my mind? Am I ready to push away from the shoreline where everything is familiar and launch out into the deep waters of uncertainty?*

I have this amazing opportunity to hide away and spend forty days alone with Jesus. Wow! Who wouldn't want to do that? It's the dream of a lifetime, and the beautiful thing is, He orchestrated all of it. This is His plan!

Yes, part of me was excited that I'd been chosen; yet another part of me was apprehensive. I'd never done anything like this before. What will this look like? What will I do throughout the day to occupy my time? Will I get bored? Will

I start talking to myself? Will I give up and turn back? All these questions were flooding my thoughts—like streams of water merging into a river, causing it to overflow its banks.

Don't misunderstand. I cherish my alone times with Jesus. I love spending precious moments together—just the two of us—but that's usually only about an hour each day, maybe two. The thought of spending forty days, hidden away with very little social contact, seems a little unsettling and even a bit scary, especially for someone who is used to interacting with people daily.

Okay, Peggy, stop it! Get out of bed. You can't allow yourself to overthink this. You've already committed, so get up. Besides, I thought, *if Jesus is asking me to go on this journey, He will give me the grace I need to walk it out, and I will benefit from it.*

Before doing anything else, I decided to take a few minutes to talk to my Beloved King:

"Jesus, here I am, stepping out in faith to go with You on this journey, a journey I've never taken before. I desire to give myself completely to You these next forty days. I don't have a plan. I don't have an agenda. I have NO IDEA what to expect. But, with blind faith, I'm trusting in You, my Beloved King, as I go and flow with Your plans for us.

"Take my hand, Jesus, and walk with me each step of this journey. Lead me through Your refining fire, if need be. I consecrate myself completely to You. Wash me. Change me. Purify me. I want it all. No turning back now. From this

moment forward, I want my life to be a living testimony that brings You glory and honor. I am yours, Lord! In Your name, Jesus. Amen."

I rolled out of bed, showered, grabbed some breakfast, finished packing, loaded my car, and left for the Great Unknown. When I say, "the Great Unknown," I mean just that. A blank slate. A formless void. A veil of secrecy.

On Our Way

"Lord, I don't know what You are about to do," I prayed as I headed south, *"but I choose to stay in peace, knowing that You have a plan. I choose to trust You. You know me, and You know the adventurer in me. So, I'm ready for this epic experience with You! Here we go!"*

The drive to my resting and nesting place in South Carolina was so inspiring. I spent most of the way in a place of stillness before the Lord, waiting and listening to hear what He wanted to reveal to me. I pondered how He had orchestrated and brought all this about. I thought about how He had shared His love for me, His Bride, over the past several days and how much He was looking forward to our time together.

The greatest desire of our Beloved King is to be with us. He will even call us to pull away for extended periods to seek Him in a deeper, more intimate place in His heart. When the invitation is extended, don't hesitate or say, "No."

Remember, when He calls, it's always for a greater purpose and for our benefit.

I then whispered, *"I am my Beloved's, and His desire is toward me"* (Song of Songs 7:10). Upon uttering those words, I could feel Him drawing me even closer.

I began to weep with joy as my heart became saturated with His presence. Waves of His glory washed over me like liquid fire, purging me. I felt as if I were in a glory bubble. I laughed. I cried. I worshipped my King and sang songs of adoration to Him as He continued to overwhelm my heart with His love. I thought to myself, *Wow! This is too good to be true! I haven't even arrived at my destination yet, and I'm already getting blasted with His glorious presence. If this is how my time with Him is going to start, then I can't imagine what the next few weeks will hold.*

After about an hour had passed, His presence lifted. My tears began to subside. As I looked in the mirror to wipe the mascara from my face, I smiled. "Thank You, Lord, for Your overwhelming love. This has been the best drive from Chattanooga to Atlanta I've ever experienced." (And I had taken that part of the trip many times.) Still, many miles stretched before us.

The "Matron" of Honor

Within a couple of hours into my trip, I received a phone call from my prayer mentor, Dr. Bob Perry, who had called to pray for me. As he was praying, Holy Spirit said, *"You already have your bridesmaids who are assigned to cover you in prayer. Now, I want you to ask Bob to be your Matron of Honor."* (Yes, you heard that right. A male *"Matron"*!)

"Why him?" I asked. "Are You sure? That seems weird since he is a guy."

"Yes, I'm sure," He replied. *"Bob has encouraged you and prayed for you to step into this next phase of your calling more than anyone else. And there is neither male nor female in the Spirit. I want you to view this from a spiritual perspective rather than a natural one."*

After the prayer time, I shared with Bob how Holy Spirit had instructed me to pick out six bridesmaids to pray for me while on the journey. "He wants them to send me any insight or encouragement they may get for me during my time away." I paused, then added, a bit hesitantly, "Holy Spirit also wants me to ask you to be my Matron of Honor."

To my surprise, he answered immediately. *"Yes! Absolutely!* I would be honored to do that!"

"*Really?* Oh, thank you, thank you!" I exclaimed. "This blesses me so much!"

When the call ended, I began to think about the people my Beloved had chosen to make up my bridal party. Bob, my Matron of Honor, represented the leadership prayer covering for me. Each of the six bridesmaids held a special place in my heart as friends, and they all had these two things in common: they loved Jesus, and they loved to pray!

I wondered why my Beloved had chosen seven rather than five, six, or even eight for the bridal party. Then I remembered the significance of the number 7 in the Scriptures. Seven signifies "perfection, completion, rest, and fulfillment of God's purposes." This gave me confidence that this journey with Him would fulfill a greater purpose than I had thought or imagined.

"Jesus, I sense that this bridal party is Your way of assuring me that I do not have to be concerned. I am completely covered in prayer by those You have selected. Lord, I am so amazed at how You are bringing all of this together. I'm not sure why, but I'm so grateful You chose me even though, at the moment, I have no idea what I've been chosen for...."

First Destination

After six hours of driving time, I finally made it to my first destination. For nine days, I would be staying in this cute little cottage-style house in Due West, South Carolina. It is an

Airbnb owned by my friends David and Bonita Hershberger. And the beautiful blessing is that my Beloved paid for it! After five years of living fully by faith, I'd come to know firsthand that where He guides, He provides.

So, with luggage in both hands and my backpack slung over my shoulders, I stepped onto the porch, took a deep breath, unlocked the front door, and walked inside. After only a few steps, I immediately dropped my bags and fell to my knees. I could feel the sweet love and weighty presence of my Beloved covering me like a bridal veil on my wedding day.

With my body in a fetal position, face down on the floor, a river of tears began to stream from my eyes. The glory of His presence was so strong, I could hardly breathe. I couldn't even get up. As I wept and wept, I said, "I can't believe this, Lord! Everywhere I go, You are there, waiting for me. Just a couple of hours ago, You filled me with Your glorious presence in my car, and now You are here in this intimate little house, waiting for me to arrive. I'm overwhelmed by Your goodness."

Once the glory cloud lifted, I finally gained the strength to pull myself up off the floor. I stood for a few moments, soaking in my surroundings. The atmosphere in the room was scented with a clean, light fragrance. All the walls were painted white, reflecting the purity of His presence.

Making my way to the bedroom, I stepped inside, feeling like a bride who had just walked into her bridal chamber. The bed was beautifully made up with a white comforter and fluffy, white pillows. Stretching out, I sank into its softness, not wanting to move. Overwhelmed once more, I couldn't stop crying.

When we allow the Lord to direct our steps, it's amazing to see how intentional He is. He gives us everything we need to fulfill His plan. That's why it is necessary to pay close attention to what He is speaking to us. Sometimes it's in the smallest details that He is revealing the most important truths.

It was the Lord who orchestrated this journey for me. He put it together, right down to the different places I would stay and His strategic purpose for me in being there. I didn't know all of this at the beginning of the journey, of course, but He did. As I trusted Him in faith and followed Him in obedience, He showed me His plans as they unfolded.

I Said "Yes!"

After a long first day, I unpacked my bags and settled in. Sitting on the sofa to catch my breath, I began to reflect on what my Beloved had shared with me on New Year's Eve. He had said, *"While others are entering 2021 with a **war** and a **roar**, I am calling you in as a Bride to **consummate** and **consecrate** yourself fully to Me."*

"Why me, Lord?" I said aloud. "Why are You asking *me?* Why am I being called to this set-apart place?"

I then heard Him say, *"Because You said YES to My call long ago."*

Once again, tears flowed freely as His presence filled my heart. Immediately, my thoughts drifted backward in time. When did I say YES to Him? How long ago? I recalled the times after my salvation experience when I had such a hunger to know the Jesus I had been reading about in the Bible. I remembered how I didn't want to settle for anything less than His all for me.

Instantly, I thought of that unforgettable day when I received what the Scriptures speak of as the "Baptism in the Holy Spirit." That's an experience I will never forget. I sat in a chair with those around me laying hands on me and praying for me. I had such a deep hunger for more of Jesus.

At that moment, I asked Him to fill me with the precious Holy Spirit. All at once, I felt as if someone had taken a pitcher of oil and poured it over my head. I could feel the warm liquid running down my face and my body. It was as if I had been immersed in His precious anointing oil. Everything in me felt so alive. I laughed and cried with excitement, feeling the joy of the Lord as it overwhelmed me. I knew that I had been anointed for a specific purpose that day, and it is forever branded in my heart.

"Is this what You are referring to, Lord? Or what about all those times, as a young girl, when I would go exploring in the nearby woods to follow the creek. I didn't know it back then, but a few years ago, You showed me that You were with

19

me during those times. You didn't want me to be alone. At that time, I didn't even know You as my Lord and Savior, yet You wanted to spend time with me anyway. Maybe that's when I said 'Yes' with my heart."

Then, of course, there were countless other experiences and encounters I have had with Him through the years when His presence would overtake me as I hungered and thirsted for more of Him. "Lord, was it during any of those times?" I asked.

I waited, but He didn't answer me. In my dialogues with Jesus from times past, I have come to realize that if it's something He feels I should know, He will tell me when the time is right.

If you desire a deeper intimacy with Jesus, I encourage you to pray this prayer with me.

"Jesus, I'm so thankful that You know me and my heart's desires. You lovingly draw me as Your Bride. Stir within me a greater hunger for more of You. Thank You for being patient with me. You don't push; instead, You lovingly work with me. You are such a gentle Savior. You have my permission to remove anything in my soul that is holding me back or hindering me from total surrender to You. Today, I give myself fully to You. What an amazing Bridegroom King You are. Thank You for being my Beloved and my Friend. Jesus, I love You."

CHAPTER 3

A Love Like No Other

As I lay in bed, not wanting to get up, I smiled as I thought about all that had taken place yesterday on my drive there and the beautifully blessed evening I had experienced with my Beloved. How His presence had filled my car and how He had revealed to me my "Matron of Honor" to add to the list of "bridesmaids" who would intercede for me while I was away.

Then I thought about how He had met me with a warm blanket of His peace as I stepped through the door of this cozy cottage. Finally, how I was saturated in the liquid love of His presence. *Will every day be like this?* I thought. *If so, this is going to be an unforgettable journey. I can't wait to see what's in store for me as I wake up each day.*

So, with a big stretch and a smile still on my face, I said, "Okay, Lord, I'm all Yours for the next 39 days. What's on Your agenda for us? What's the plan? Are we staying here, or are we going to visit someone? I'm listening."

You see, these are questions we often ask when we've cultivated a long season of *doing* for the Lord instead of *being* with Him. When I say *doing* for Him, I'm referring to the habit of falling into a routine of constantly serving and fulfilling the work of ministry instead of allowing intimacy with the Lord to be our top priority.

Even though in the past, I had enjoyed precious times with Him, in this season of my life, I had been more engaged in ministry activity. However, I would soon discover that before I can be effective in ministry, He wants to teach me how to *be* once again, but in a whole new and different sense.

As soon as I spoke the words, "I'm listening," I heard Him say, *"Be holy—a call to holiness."*

With that divine response, He had my full attention. "What do You mean, Lord, when You say, 'Be holy?' What is a call to holiness? What does that look like? How do we attain it?" As I asked these questions, I knew in my heart that He would not answer me directly. I knew His desire was for me to press in and search the Scriptures for myself.

What Is Holiness?

The two Scriptures I felt prompted to read are found in 1 Peter and the Book of Hebrews:

"As He who called you is holy, you also be holy in all your conduct, because it is written, 'Be holy, for I am holy.'"
~1 Peter 1:15-16

"Pursue peace with all men, and holiness, Without which no one will see the Lord."
~Hebrews 12:14

Many times, we can read Scriptures like these without taking the time to search out the meaning of the words that have been highlighted to us. In the Bible, we have been asked to study to show ourselves approved (see 2 Timothy 2:15) and to meditate on the Scriptures and not just skim them quickly.

Since I was asked by my Beloved to *"be holy"* and there was a *"call to holiness,"* I figured I should at least gain a better understanding of what was being required of me through a deeper study of these words.

Being holy is not just something we acquire by what we do. According to Hebrews 10:10, we have been made holy *"by the offering of the body of Jesus Christ once for all."* In the Book of Ephesians, we are told that God *"has raised us up together, and made us sit together in the heavenly places in Christ Jesus"* (2:6). So, if we are "in

23

Christ," as far as our spiritual position in Him, we are holy. However, in our earthly soul and body, we are to walk out being holy by drawing near to Jesus and being obedient to Him in all that we do, say, and think. We grow in holiness as we continue to spend time with Him in prayer and the reading of His Word.

Let's look at the word *holy* in 1 Peter 1:15, which is the Greek word *hagios,* meaning: "a moral quality; to be consecrated (set apart) and acceptable to God." This word is a call to action on our part, specifically in our conduct— the way we behave. When we decide to give Jesus our all, He begins the sanctification process.

The word *holiness* in Hebrews 12:14 is the Greek word *hagiasmos,* meaning "sanctification or to set apart for special use or purpose." In this verse, we are asked to pursue peace, but we are also to pursue holiness. To *pursue* is "to actively and diligently chase after something with determination and consistent effort."

The benefit of pursuing holiness is seeing God! This benefit is not bestowed when we get to heaven only, but it is for *now,* while we are still earthbound! We can see Him in the beauty of *His* holiness.

As I think about these two words, *holy and holiness,* I am reminded once again of the two words spoken to me a couple of days before: *consecrate* and *consummate.* As I shared in the previous chapter, to *consecrate* is "to set apart; to dedicate to a sacred purpose; to make or declare sacred."

To *consummate* is "to make complete (through intimacy) in every detail; perfect, extremely skilled, and accomplished."

To be holy is part of the consecration process. Once we consecrate (set apart) our hearts fully to Jesus, He can lead us through the consummation process, where He reveals and removes the impurities within us so that we can accomplish His plans and purpose for our lives. This call to holiness is not a one-time deal but an ongoing work.

When we ask Holy Spirit to help us in consecrating ourselves to the Lord, He will begin to search our hearts and reveal the hidden things in our lives that hinder us from experiencing a deeper intimacy with Jesus and also affect our relationship with others. In Song of Songs, those "hidden things" are called "little foxes."

"Those Sly Little Foxes"

"You must catch the troubling foxes, those sly
little foxes that hinder our relationship.
For they raid our budding vineyard of love
to ruin what I've planted within you.
Will you catch them and remove them for me?
We will do it together."
~Song of Songs 2:15, TPT

Our Bridegroom King longs to take us into a deeper experience of knowing Him and His heart. When we submit to His process of removing the *"troubling and sly little foxes"* —those hidden things buried deep in our souls, such as anger, bitterness, rejection, fear, etc.—then we can be effective as vessels He can flow through. The beauty of this process is that He reveals and removes the hidden things from us one at a time; and we get to do this together with our Beloved King. That's when we begin to experience Him and His love for us in a new and more profound way.

Have you ever been sitting with the Lord, enjoying your time with Him, when suddenly, out of nowhere, He highlights a specific weakness you didn't even realize was there? Or maybe it's something you have struggled with in the past but thought you had overcome or been delivered from.

Well, this is exactly what happened to me.

While meditating on holiness in my quiet time, I asked the Lord, "If there are any 'sly little foxes' within me, please reveal them and heal any secret areas in my soul that have been wounded." Sure enough, He did just that! (Remember, we get what we ask for!)

Around midday, I received an email from someone who corrected me because of something they thought I had done for them incorrectly. Immediately, I felt an offense rise up followed by feelings of rejection—like a dagger piercing my heart. I could feel myself getting a little angry and irritated.

As I stewed over this for a bit, I thought to myself, *Maybe I should respond. Maybe I should ask, "Why are you correcting me? Remember, I was helping you out! And at the last minute at that!"*

Just as I was about to send that message, instead of reacting, I sensed the need to pause and inquire of Holy Spirit what was going on within me.

"Why did I get offended?" I asked Him. "Why am I feeling rejected? I thought I had already dealt with rejection in the past and was free from it." He was silent. I kept listening and waiting, but no answer.

Taking a deep breath, I said, "Okay, Lord, I give You permission to help me identify the root cause as to why I allowed myself to pick up an offense and feel rejected." (In His tender grace, our Beloved will not expose our deep wounds or hurts if we are not ready to address or deal with them.)

I then heard Him say, *"Your identity."*

What? My identity? *Ouch!* I wasn't expecting that to be the problem.

"You don't fully know who you are in Me," He continued. *"You have been finding your identity in what you DO for Me instead of who you ARE in Me."*

Oh, wow! That was an eye-opener. I had no idea I had allowed what I do for Him to become my identity. I asked Him for forgiveness right away! I did not want my "works" to define who I am in Him. Instead, I want my identity to be in who I am as His beloved Bride and daughter of the Most High God.

If you are struggling with the issue of identity, I want to encourage you to pray this prayer of permission with me so that Holy Spirit can reveal anything that is keeping you from knowing who you are in Christ Jesus.

Prayer of Permission:

"Jesus, forgive me for having the wrong view of myself. From this moment forward, I permit You to reveal the things in my soul that are hindering me from knowing who I am in You. No matter how painful, please reveal them so that we can deal with them together. I want to be healed, delivered, and walk in the freedom of knowing who I am in You as my Bridegroom and King."

Rejection can enter our souls through many different avenues, experiences, and seasons in our lives. Most often, it comes in at a weak or vulnerable moment in time, especially during childhood. If we do not receive the healing that is needed, woundedness can become a stronghold. This will hinder our relationship with other people, with Jesus, and with our heavenly Father.

Even though we may have dealt with a specific area in our past and received healing, there can still be other areas we haven't recognized or been shown by Holy Spirit. Once He reveals these areas, we must ask Him to show us what is needed to bring healing so that we can receive the freedom to move forward.

Our Language of Love

While sitting in stillness, waiting, and resting with my Beloved, I was amazed at how much peace I was experiencing. No talking, just listening for His voice. He then began to share with me different songs He knew I loved. Songs to help tenderize my heart in preparation for a greater depth of experiencing His presence.

That's the beauty of taking the necessary time to listen and communicate with our Beloved. He knows our language of love. If you are unsure of your personal love language with the Lord, ask Him, and then pay attention to the things that stir your heart and draw you closer to Him.

As for me, He knows that song lyrics are one of my favorite languages of love. Words and phrases such as *I love you, adoration, ravish* ("fill with intense delight"), *majesty,* and *passion* reveal to me His beauty, captivate my heart, and draw me deeper into intimacy and worship of Him.

He knows that certain frequencies in the sound of music prepare my heart for His presence to come in. Like the longing, intimate voice of the violin. Or the gentle strumming of the acoustic guitar. Or the beautiful melodies of the keyboard. These are the ways He draws me so that I will pursue Him. In return, He will lavish ("release in abundance") His presence upon me.

He will also share specific Scriptures with me. Scriptures that I have meditated on over the years. Scriptures that speak tenderly from His heart to mine:

> *"For you reach into my heart with one flash of your eyes. I am undone by your love, My Beloved, My equal, My Bride.*
> *You leave me breathless—I am overcome by merely a glance from your worshipping eyes for you have captured My heart. I am held hostage by your love and by the graces of righteousness shining upon you"*
> ~Song of Songs 4:9, TPT

As I worshipped and adored Him, I began to weep. I could feel Him drawing me closer to Himself. I wept and wept in His overwhelming presence as He covered me with His banner of love. I could feel in this deep, intimate time with Him that He was bringing healing to my soul and my wounded heart from the rejection. Nothing compares with the joy of experiencing the lavish love of our King.

After my time of worship, I felt Him prompting me to watch one of the older Esther movies. I knew He had a purpose for this, even though I had no clue what it was. So, with my eyes glued to my laptop screen, I paid close attention to see what He might reveal to me. Throughout the movie, I could sense a beautiful display of love from my Bridegroom

King for me. My heart became even more moved by His tender affection.

When the movie ended, one of the statements that captured my attention was a prophetic utterance from Mordecai to Esther: *"Yet who knows whether you have been brought to the kingdom for such a time as this?"* (Esther 4:14). So, that was it! That's what He wanted to reveal to me! But why?

I then remembered receiving this same Scripture from one of my bridesmaids earlier in the day. Later in this journey, I would discover why this particular Scripture was given to me. Now I know that I am to be alert for messages that come to me unexpectedly. "Jesus, I'm watching and listening...."

Good Night Prayer:

"Thank You, my Beloved King, for another amazing day with You. Thank You for confirming Your Word and revealing the areas in my soul that still need to be healed. Thank You for visiting me and showering me with Your beautiful love. I will lie down in peace and sleep, knowing that You are ever watching over me. Good night, my King."

CHAPTER 4

Refrain from Distractions

*"And this I say for your own profit,
not that I may put a leash on you,
but for what is proper, and that you
may serve the Lord without distraction."*

~1 Corinthians 7:35

I n the first week of my time away with the Lord, I was forced to navigate a major hindrance. This hindrance affects all of us. Some struggle with it more than others, but we are all impacted in some way. As you will see later in this chapter, what I am referring to is *distractions*.

The first thing I did when I woke up the next morning was to reach for my phone to see if any texts had come in. (Old habits are hard to break!) To my surprise, I had received a link to a song, "God Finds Us," sent by one of my bridesmaids. Eager to hear what she had selected for me, I sat up in bed, put my head back, and closed my eyes as I began to listen. The sounds from the instruments brought peace and rest to my body, mind, and spirit. The lyrics ministered to me deeply, bringing comfort and reassurance that my Beloved was with me in every situation.

I love how He constantly drops little nuggets along the way to feed us and encourage us as we draw closer to Him. He does this so that we will continue to press in to hear His heart and what He is saying to us. As I shared with you earlier, He gave me "bridesmaids"—intercessors—not only to pray for me but to encourage me on my journey. He does not show favoritism. If He did this for me, He will do it for you.

I listened to the song over and over as if it were a necessary meal that would sustain me throughout the day. Suddenly, out of nowhere, I heard my Beloved whisper, *"It is simple."*

"Jesus, what do you mean?" I asked. *"What* is simple? I don't understand."

"Don't make it so complicated. Wait. Listen. Don't get in a hurry. Quiet your soul. This is a time to wait and meditate. Go back if you must and review. It's about listening, watching, and waiting."

After hearing those words, I still wasn't completely sure what He was saying to me, but I was confident that He would bring complete clarity in His timing. I felt this would be a day of instruction from Him, so I decided to spend the rest of my day paying close attention to what was going on around me.

Nature Speaks

It was a chilly South Carolina day, but I felt the need to leave the house and get some fresh air. As much as I dislike the cold, I decided to go for a nature walk anyway. I love hiking and exploring. My Beloved knows this about me, of course, and when we go for walks, He speaks to me through the sights and sounds of the natural world.

So, I bundled up, and off I went down the narrow, gravel road near the place where I was staying. It was wintertime, so there wasn't much activity in the woods. I had to listen closely to hear what nature was saying to me. The wind was gently blowing through the barren trees. It's as if they were whispering, *"Hello!"* to me in their own unique language as they swayed in the breeze.

I heard the occasional chirping of birds in the far-off distance, reminding me of how much I missed the warm spring weather and looked forward to its return. I also heard squirrels scratching through the fallen leaves, looking for any acorns that may have been left behind from the fall harvest. I felt the Lord fine-tuning my spiritual antennae as I sensed deep within my soul a greater depth of healing taking place.

Throughout the rest of the day, I made it a point to wait, listen, and pay close attention to what Holy Spirit wanted to reveal to me. I became more aware of the sights and sounds around me. My spiritual senses were becoming more awakened as I quieted my soul.

Letting Go

With each passing day, I discovered how difficult it was for me to tune out the noise of the world. You would think by now I would have turned off my phone, but for some reason, I was having a hard time doing that. As an intercessor, I like to keep it close by me. It's my connection with the outside world, and it helps me to have a better understanding of what is going on so I will know how to pray.

You are probably wondering, "But I thought you were on this journey to let go of the outside world and spend time alone with Jesus?" Well, that was my original intent. However, there is a process in walking out one's calling. It takes time and trust to let go of the familiar and step into the unknown. I'm so thankful our Beloved King is patient with us and doesn't rush us when it is time to let go.

In Proverbs 3:5-6 we are instructed: *"Trust in the Lord with all your heart, and do not lean on your own understanding. In all your ways acknowledge Him, and He will direct your paths."*

Distractions, whether good or bad, can be a huge stumbling block to our spiritual growth and God's direction for our lives. They are often used by the enemy to take us off the path of God's choosing, and if we aren't careful, they can lead us into deception. They hinder us from trusting the Lord and cause us to look at the circumstances around us instead of leaning on the One who can lead us in and through our circumstances. If we do not rely on Holy Spirit for guidance and help, God's plans and purposes for our lives can be delayed or thwarted altogether.

Distractions come from many directions and for different reasons. One way is through our thoughts. When we are committed to a certain task or assignment, our thoughts can easily take us off course. Every thought imaginable may come to mind. But God's Word encourages us to *"take every thought captive to the obedience of Christ"* (2 Corinthians 10:5). In other words, we must examine our thoughts and ensure that they align with His Word and His character.

Social media, television, phone calls—all forms of communication and technology—can easily distract us in this high-tech culture. Then there are our family, friends, neighbors, and co-workers. The list goes on. Some of these distractions are part of our day-to-day life and are good and necessary. Others come because we allow them, and still others originate from spiritual forces of darkness that deliberately set out to lead us down the wrong path. We have the power and authority through Holy Spirit to forbid them to hinder us. If we do not deal with distractions, they will continue to slow down the process of completing what we set out to accomplish. Sometimes, though, we allow distractions because they are a cover-up for the real issues in our lives— issues that we haven't dealt with. That's what I realized was happening in my life.

My biggest distraction on my journey thus far was my cell phone. (You might want to ask Holy Spirit to show *you* the things that are distracting *you* from accomplishing His purpose for your life.)

My Confession:

"My Beloved, I must admit, my fear is that if I shut off my phone, I will be isolated—maybe even forgotten by others. I will be by myself with no one to talk to. I am not quite ready for that step yet. I know that will be necessary eventually, and I'm going to need Your help. But for now… well, the phone gives me a sense of comfort and security. I know I am to keep my focus on You and shut out what's going on in the world, but it's not easy. I'm constantly being distracted by emails and people sending texts to let me know what's happening in our world.

If I can be honest with You, I desire to be out there praying with everyone else. I don't feel I'm doing my part, hidden away like this. I know this is a great opportunity, and many Christians would love to be in my place. However, this is a huge struggle for me. I feel torn between ministering in the outside world and being here with You. I know Your desire is for us to be together in solitude, and deep in my heart, it's my desire, too. Yet, the struggle is real. I need Your help, Lord. No matter how I'm feeling, I choose to stay here with You."

I then heard my Beloved say: *"Why do you want to go 'out there'? What is your purpose? Is it to be seen of man? Is it because that's what everyone else is doing? My Bride, you must understand that it's in Me you live, move, and have your being. Apart from Me, you can do nothing, but in Me, with Me, and through Me, you can do all things. Think not that you can't be just as effective here, IN ME, as you can out there. Your obedience to stay here with Me will produce more than your disobedience in the world. I'm calling you IN, so I can teach you how to be more effective when you are sent back OUT. Be still and war with Me from the Secret Place."*

"Jesus, I repent of my soulish desires. Running to battle in prayer and intercession with everyone else is what I've done for so long, so it seems unnatural not to do that. As I'm discovering, though, You desire to teach me a more excellent way."

*"Once again, Peggy, I'm calling you to lead by example and to **refrain from distractions!**"*

Without even realizing it, our relationship with Jesus can easily get pushed to the side. We get caught up in following the crowd, serving and working for Him, and we forget about our Bride-Bridegroom intimacy that must be cultivated through spending time with Him *first,* before anything else. *Being with Him* should always come before *doing for Him.*

Pursuing Jesus

That afternoon, I went for another long walk in some nearby woods. The quiet, peaceful sights and sounds of nature helped me to shut down the distractions that were bombarding my thoughts earlier.

While walking, I came across a beautiful flowing stream with a large rock situated nearby. As I sat there watching the water ripple over the rocks, I was reminded of one of my favorite Scriptures: *"He shall be like a tree planted by the rivers of water, that brings forth its fruit in its season, whose leaf also shall not wither; And whatever he does shall prosper"* (Psalm 1:3).

I lay back against the rock, closed my eyes, and meditated on what it would be like to be a tree planted by the rivers of His *living* water. As I listened to the rushing stream, I could feel the healing warmth of the sun on my face. In this moment, there was so much peace and freedom.

By that night, although I did my best to focus on my Beloved—reading and studying His Word—I continued to receive texts from other intercessors, sharing with me the arrests, riots, and chaos in our nation's capital and throughout the country. So much division. So much hatred. Political differences. Racial tensions. I felt such a burden in my soul that I spent over an hour weeping and crying out to the Lord in prayer. This remained heavy on my heart for the rest of the night, and I cried myself to sleep.

A Different Perspective

I tossed and turned all night, wrestling in prayer, and woke up the next morning exhausted. Sitting up in bed, I blinked in the bright morning sunlight streaming through the window.

When I could open my eyes fully, I got up, fixed myself a cup of coffee, and crawled back into bed, anticipating hearing from my Beloved. Suddenly, I felt Him draw near.

"Last night, did you intercede from your soul or from what you know to be true?" He asked gently.

As I took a moment to ponder what He had said, I realized that He was asking this question to teach me a key lesson in intercession. So, I took a deep breath and replied honestly, "From my soul."

In that instant, I knew that I had allowed the distractions of current events to bring unrest to my mind, which affected my soul. This took me to a place of doubt and confusion instead of remaining in faith and trust. Once I allowed this to happen, my intercession was hindered. Instead of believing and trusting by faith the promises in God's Word, I had become moved by the circumstances around me. This is praying from the soul, which causes intercession to be ineffective.

When we intercede from what we know to be God's truth, we see the circumstances around us, but we are not moved by them. Instead, we ask Holy Spirit to reveal heaven's perspective. Then we can pray, decree, or declare the promises found in His Word according to the will of our Heavenly Father.

> *"Now this is the confidence that we have in Him, that if we ask anything according to His will, He hears us. And if we know that He hears us, whatever we ask, we know that we have the petitions that we have asked of Him."*
> ~1 John 5:14-15

I took some time to sit with my Beloved to reflect on what He had shared with me. "Lord," I began, "is this what You meant when You spoke to me back in December and said, *'I'm pulling you out of prayer, as **you know it?'*** If so, I want to know more. Give me insight. Teach me Your way. This is something I haven't heard of or been a part of on my previous prayer journey."

I then heard Him say, *"Trust Me."*

It's not always easy to trust an outcome when you have no idea what the end result will be or the steps necessary to get there. That's where faith comes in. Our faith comes from trusting our heavenly Bridegroom even when it seems impossible. We must trust that He is always with us, looking out for us, and has His best for us in mind.

True faith in Him is when we trust, even in the unseen. We develop and grow in our faith over time as we get to know Him. If we don't know Him, we can't trust Him.

Acclimating My Spirit

I awoke the next morning, thinking about the past few days of the journey. To be honest, I didn't feel I'd done very well. It's as if I kept stumbling over the same obstacle each day.

I asked myself, *Why is it so difficult for me to let go of what I can't change? Why can't I just shut my phone off? And when I do, why do I keep thinking about what might be happening while I'm here, hidden away from everything and everyone?*

Thank God this wasn't a real test, or I would have failed miserably. I'm so grateful for the patience my Beloved was showing me while I walked through new territory.

Leaving all that was familiar to be alone with Jesus had been more difficult than I thought it would be. What I was being called to was deeper than I realized. It wasn't just going away to spend time with Him. He was calling me to fully surrender my will to His will for me. To learn to rest in Him, lean on Him, and abandon myself completely to Him in every area of my life. Even though it was not easy, I was determined to keep moving forward.

In that dear and familiar voice, I heard Him say, *"Peggy, it will not benefit you to hang onto the old. You can't bring into the new season what you have previously been a part of in the old season. If anything, it will become a weight and a hindrance to slow you down or even to halt your progress altogether."*

Then I remembered what Jesus had said in the Scriptures about putting new wine into old wineskins. He said the new wine would burst the old wineskin, the wine would spill out, and the wineskin would be ruined. But new wine must be put into new wineskins. (See Mark 2:22.)

What a great reminder that when it's time for an assignment or season in our life to change, go in a different direction, or completely end, we must allow Holy Spirit to help us let go. He knows how to nudge us, reminding us to start freeing ourselves of the things that are to be removed. They are the things that will no longer serve us in the next season. If anything, they will hinder, slow us down, or stop His plan for us altogether.

I want my Bridegroom King to do whatever is necessary in me so that I will come forth as the Shulamite in Song of Songs 8:5: *"Who is this coming up out of the wilderness leaning on her Beloved?"*

At that point, I contacted one of my bridesmaids to pray for me regarding the distractions and the struggle to let go of the familiar. She sent this word to me: "God is acclimating your spirit."

To *acclimate* is "to become accustomed to a new climate or new conditions. To adapt or adjust to something new." *Wow, spot on! Yes, that is exactly what He is doing,* I thought. *I see now why I am experiencing such a struggle and tug-of-war in my soul.*

And not knowing anything else to do, I reached out to the One who *does* know: *"Jesus, thank You for walking with me in this time of acclimation. I feel like one of the children of Israel who circled the same mountain (obstacles) repeatedly, yet You are so faithful, gentle, and kind in Your patience with me. You don't get angry with me. You tenderly speak to me, giving me instructions as You show me areas of my soul that need healing and renewal. For this I am grateful. Good night, my Beloved. I love You."*

CHAPTER 5
The Invitation

"For you reach into my heart,
With one flash of your eyes
I am undone by your love,
My beloved, my equal, my Bride.
You leave me breathless—--
I am overcome
by merely a glance from
your worshipping eyes,
for you have stolen my heart.
I am held hostage by your love
and by the graces of
righteousness shining upon you."

~Song of Songs 4:9

There are appointed times with our beloved King when He extends an invitation for us to do something else we've never done before. Something that truly takes us out of our normal routine with Him. An out-of-the-box experience, so to speak. One that could appear radical if shared with others who might not have an understanding of the depth of Jesus' love for His Bride. He wants to see if we will step out in faith to honor His request. Will we set aside our reservations to respond to His desires, no matter what it feels like or looks like to others?

When the Lord invites us to do what feels uncomfortable or different, we should accept His invitation. Our obedience becomes a beautiful display of our passionate love for our Bridegroom King. In return, He will lavish us with the fragrant oil of His love.

Earlier in the week, I had felt prompted by my Beloved to have a date night with Him as Bridegroom and Bride. Although He had never asked me anything like this before, I quickly agreed. "Absolutely! How amazing is this? A date night with *You,* Jesus? What would that even look like? What would we do? Where would we go? What do I wear? What night did You have in mind?"

I knew He was listening to my questions and would answer all of them at the appointed time. And He did!

His request was for me to prepare a meal for the two of us. We would eat together on Friday night, and after our meal, we would take communion. The menu would be my choice, even though I had no idea what I should choose. I felt everything else would flow naturally once I started to prepare for the evening.

A Night to Remember

On Friday afternoon, I looked at the time and realized I had only a couple of hours before my date with the King. Not knowing what to expect, I was both nervous and excited. Even with the anxiety, though, I sensed that this was going to be a night I would always cherish.

Jumping into my car, I dashed off to the grocery store to get the food to prepare for our dinner. This was all new to me, so I wasn't exactly sure what to purchase. I hadn't prepared a meal for a date in a long time, but I knew whatever I chose would be perfect for my honored Guest. Jesus is so gracious and understanding.

Personally, I don't require anything fancy, at least not if I'm doing the cooking! I decided on chicken as the main dish. You can't go wrong with chicken prepared with olive oil, salt, and pepper. I also bought salad fixings, bread, sweet potatoes, and a bottle of wine. Wine is not something I normally drink, except on special occasions, but I felt it was particularly appropriate for this meal and our future times of communion. I also bought some flowers and a candle for the table.

When I got back from the grocery store, I put on some soft, instrumental worship music to set the tone for the atmosphere in the room. Then I began to prepare the food. I put the sweet potatoes in the oven to bake, fixed a tasty salad, and diced the chicken to sauté in olive oil over low heat.

While the food was cooking, I went to my room to get dressed. I had brought a couple of dressy outfits with me just in case I had the opportunity to go to church while I was there. I put on make-up and lipstick, then curled my hair. I wanted to look my best for my King, even though I knew my outward appearance didn't matter to Him. He would be looking past the visible to the invisible condition of my heart.

Slipping on some low-heeled shoes, I went to the dining room and set the table for two. I turned off all the lights except for a small lamp in the living room. Then I lit the candles on the table for an intimate atmosphere for our meal and arranged the bread and wine for communion. When the food was ready, I placed it on the table. "Perfect," I said softly, knowing He would agree.

Taking my seat, I looked across the table at the place I had set for my Beloved. Feeling a little awkward, I attempted to start the conversation. "So … here we are, Jesus. What would You like to talk about?"

I could feel His pleasure in being invited to this intimate dinner, and I heard Him say to my heart, *"Peggy, You are so beautiful!"*

Immediately, tears filled my eyes and began to trickle down my cheeks. I could feel the tenderness of His love as it wrapped around me like a warm hug. His presence filled the room. He was so gentle, yet the power of His love took my breath away.

But there were more endearing words of affirmation. *"Peggy, I love You just the way you are!"*

At that, I burst into tears, unable to hold them back any longer. The sound of His voice speaking those words to my heart caused all the insecurities I had felt throughout the week to melt away. It was as if they had never existed.

He whispered to me, *"Play that song by Billy Joel,' I Love You Just the Way You Are.'"* (Yes, the Lord also uses secular music to speak to us.)

With trembling hands, I reached for my phone. As the tears continued to spill over, I finally found the song on YouTube. I listened intently to every word, and it was as if my Beloved was the voice singing the song specifically to me.

I wept and wept as the lyrics swept over my heart like ocean waves crashing onto a California shoreline. I could feel each word wash over me, bringing deep healing to my soul. His glorious presence was so overwhelming that I couldn't speak. Nor did I need to speak. Our hearts were so intertwined that words were unnecessary.

I laid my head on the table, unable to control my weeping. It felt as if my head were pressed against His chest, and I could feel His heart beating with mine. I could feel Him stroking my hair with His hand and tenderly caressing my face with His fingers. The moment was so sublime that I didn't want to move for fear it would end.

All at once, tears of joy burst forth like a geyser. And I laughed and laughed, while tears streamed down my cheeks. I couldn't contain myself. This is what I like to call, "Holy Ghost Presence Laughter and Tears." In that moment, all I wanted was to remain near Him and feel His warm, liquid love pouring over every part of my heart.

Communing with My King

I was in no hurry to end this part of our special evening. In these moments with Him, I knew beyond any doubt how much He truly loved me, flaws and all. I didn't have to pretend with Him. I could be myself because, apparently, although He knew everything about me, He still wanted to be with me. He was willing to walk with me through the necessary steps to overcome whatever was holding me back from going deeper with Him.

I knew I had just experienced the revelation found in Song of Songs 7:10: *"Now I know that I am for my Beloved and all His desires are fulfilled in me"* (TPT).

After dinner, we took Communion together. This was the most intimate moment of all as we joined hearts and souls in remembering my Lord's great sacrifice of love for me— and for you.

Partaking of Communion is the most sacred act that we, as followers of Christ, can do as we remember His sacrifice on the cross. Jesus gave His life to redeem us from the power of sin and death and restore us to God as sons and daughters. (If possible, put this book aside and pause to partake of Communion to remember the body and blood of our Lord and Savior, Jesus Christ.)

Communion Prayer:

"Jesus, You took the bread that represents Your body and blessed it. Lord, sanctify this bread that I hold in my hand to be what You said it is—Your body. I receive and partake of Your body and ask that You live Your life in and through me.

Jesus, You, took the cup that represents Your blood, lifted it, and blessed it. Lord, sanctify this cup to be what you said it is—Your blood. As I receive and partake of Your blood, I ask that its power flow in and through me. I ask this in Your name. Amen."

Reflections

I lay in bed the next morning, pondering all that had taken place with my Beloved the previous night. I can't even express in words what our evening together meant to me. That intimate encounter with the King of all kings was an experience I will always remember and forever cherish. I felt as if the Lover of all lovers was romancing me. Not in a worldly way but in a spiritual, heart-to-heart encounter between Bride and Bridegroom.

I rolled over in bed, sat up, and heard these words from my Beloved: *"Come away with Me."*

Immediately my heart leapt! "What? Did you just ask me to come away with You? Absolutely! Yes! Yes, Lord, You know I will. That's what I desire more than anything. I want to come away with You, my Beloved, King. But where are we going?"

When the Lord extends this type of invitation, it is usually to draw us unto Himself and to prepare us for a greater purpose. He is waiting and listening to hear us say, "YES, Lord, I will answer Your call."

Jesus said in Matthew 22:14, *"For many are called, but few [will pay the price to be]... chosen"* (author insertion).

As I sat still before my Beloved and meditated on what He had just said to me, I asked, "Jesus, what did you mean when You said, 'Come away with Me?' I thought that's what I am here for—to come away with You. Can you be a little more specific?"

I then heard the whisper of these lyrics of a song that so perfectly embodied what He was desiring of me, *"Come away with Me! Come away with Me! It's gonna be wild, it's gonna be great, it's gonna be for you."*

As I listened to this song, I felt myself being drawn by His presence into a deeper place of peace and rest in Him as well as a growing excitement. I could sense another invitation being extended to go to a *new* place in Him—a place of wisdom and wonder. A new level of intimacy and trust. I would be listening, watching, and waiting to see what my Beloved revealed.

> *"Jesus said to them, 'Come away with me.*
> *Let us go up to a quiet place and get some rest.'"*
> ~Mark 6:31b

Chapter 6
Enter into His Faith-Rest

*"Those who first heard the good news of deliverance
failed to enter into that realm of faith's rest because of
their unbelieving hearts. Yet the fact remains
that we still have the opportunity to enter
into the faith-rest life and experience
the fulfillment of the promise!"*
—Hebrews 4:6, TPT

Entering the second week with my Beloved King, I couldn't help reflecting on all that took place the previous week. I was still blown away by how much I had allowed myself to become distracted by the disruption in our nation caused by the COVID-19 pandemic and the presidential election. I had no idea that those events affected me so drastically. It had taken me a whole week to settle my mind and let go of the need to *do for the Lord* instead of to simply *be with Him.*

I was having to learn that living from a place of rest is an unending journey. While walking through this process with me, you will understand how I came to experience a joy and peace that I had never known before as I discovered the concept of God's faith-rest. Moving forward, I am more determined than ever to put all this unrest behind me so I can fix my gaze upon my Beloved and His desire for me.

"Jesus, show me the value of entering Your rest, and give me insight as I learn how to do so. I give myself fully to You. Help me to let go of all that hinders me from experiencing a deeper place of rest and intimacy in my relationship with You. I ask this in Your precious name. Amen."

Resting in the Beloved

While on my journey, I was learning that faith and trust are keys to unlock a lifestyle of rest. You may be asking the same question I was asking, "What is a 'lifestyle of rest' when our lives are busier than ever these days?" Before I answer that question, I'd like to share what this kind of rest is *not*. It is not sleeping till noon or lazing around on the couch all day. Although sleep and relaxation are considered forms of rest and are necessary when done properly, they are not the kind of rest I am referring to.

According to Hebrews 4:11, this is a rest that we *labor* to enter. In this case, the word labor does not mean "to work or to strive." The word *labor* in Greek means "to be eager, to make every effort, to do one's best, to be diligent." This rest is so valuable that we are to pursue it eagerly, diligently, intentionally, and no matter the cost.

So, what is the meaning of this kind of rest? It is "to keep from, to restrain, to cease from striving, to remain in peace, to have faith, to trust." To enter this rest, we must continue to cultivate an intimate relationship with Jesus—knowing *Him*, not just knowing *about* Him. As we practice the disciplines of worship, prayer, Bible reading, and letting go of distractions, our faith will increase and our trust in Him will grow.

> *"For those of us who believe, faith activates the promise (of entering into God's rest) and we experience the realm of confident rest."*
> ~Hebrews 4:3a, TPT

There is also a rest we can experience as we allow Jesus to free us from the burdens of life. In Matthew 11:28, He tells us that those who are weary and burdened are to come to Him, and He will give them **"rest."** This type of rest is "to be refreshed, rejuvenated, reinvigorated, and revitalized." We are not to worry or become heavy-laden with the troublesome issues of life, but by faith, we are to cast our concerns on Him because He cares for us (see 1 Peter 5:7).

The Lord knows when we are overwhelmed by our circumstances or just struggling with a heavy workload. We must pay attention when He nudges us to pause, pull back, and rest. If we do, we will be strengthened and encouraged.

Another form of rest, found in Genesis 2, is called a **"Sabbath rest."** This word means, "stop." In Genesis 1, we learn that God created mankind on the sixth day and rested—

"stopped"—from all His labor on the seventh day. He did this as an example to teach us the importance of rest. The significance for us is that after man was created, his first full day in the Garden was a day of rest. On the Hebraic calendar, God begins each day at sundown so that we can rest during the nighttime hours before our work begins the next morning. If our heavenly Father saw the need to create a day specifically for rest, then we should do our best to honor Him on that day.

Rest is also one of the highest forms of **spiritual warfare.** When we rest in our Beloved King, we stand in full assurance that He not only goes before us to fight our battles but is victorious over our enemies.

> *"As we enter into God's faith-rest life, we cease from our own works, just as God celebrates His finished works and rests in them."*
> ~Hebrews 4:10, TPT

Today, I find myself feeling more at peace with less stress and anxiety from what may or may not be happening in the world around me. I'm shutting off my phone and not engaging in social media or checking emails as often. Instead, I'm focusing more on reading and meditating on God's written Word. This is necessary if I want to increase my hunger to know my Beloved at a deeper level of faith and trust.

Time spent with Jesus should be our top priority, considered precious and sacred. We should treat this time as the priceless treasure it is and not waste it. Remember, once the hours and minutes are gone, they cannot be retrieved.

Spending more time with Him is what I must do to stay close to His heart and fellowship with Him. If being with Him means sacrificing my time in other areas and activities, I will gladly do it. He is worthy!

Seek Him Early

King David said it so well: *"O God, You are my God; early will I seek You; my soul thirsts for You; my flesh longs for You in a dry and thirsty land where there is no water"* (Psalm 63:1).

I love this Psalm because it has always been the cry and longing of my heart. It speaks of a personal relationship with the Living God—*"O God, You are **my** God"*—and refers to two of the major necessities of life—food and water. And right in the middle of that verse, we have the declaration: *"Early will I seek You."*

These words have been a key component of my time with the Lord. I have found that my day goes much better when I give Him the first fruits. When I get up early after a night of rest, my mind is free of the thoughts about events that have taken place during the day. In the early morning hours, I receive more clarity when I read and meditate on His Word. My worship time isn't hindered, and my time of prayer is more focused. It is during these moments with Him that I am learning how to enter into the faith-rest that my King has longed for me to experience.

If you are not already setting aside time with Jesus in the first and freshest part of your day, I encourage you to do so. Maybe set your alarm at least thirty minutes to an hour earlier than you normally do. It is also helpful to get out of bed to sit with Him. No distractions. No demands. Just you and Jesus. If you make it a priority to put Him first each day, you will discover the peace and rest He longs to give you.

If Jesus felt it necessary to seek His heavenly Father early in the mornings, then we, as His Bride, should make an effort to do the same.

Restore to Me Your Wonder

As I was sitting quietly one morning, waiting to hear what my King longed to share, He reminded me of some words He had spoken to me in August of 2020: *"I want to restore to you My wonder."* I clearly remembered that astonishing statement but had not pursued its meaning. Now, months later, He was bringing it back to my remembrance, and this time He had my full attention.

Hearing these familiar words again, my spirit began to leap. With childlike faith, I exclaimed, "Oh, Jesus, I love this! Yes, yes, restore to me Your wonder! I want to experience all that You have for me!" I paused, then asked, "But … what is Your wonder?"

I didn't get a response, which isn't unusual. As I stated previously, the Lord will sometimes present a question or idea but not always the full revelation. When that happens, I know He is either wanting me to search out the answer for myself or to wait on His timing. Since my answer didn't come right away, I decided to go for a walk in the nearby woods to meditate on the "wonder of God" and how it might appear to me.

When the Scriptures speak of "wonder," they are referring to something *supernatural*—"above the natural" or a *marvel*—"something incredible to see; a miracle." The wonder of God invites us into the realms of both the natural and the supernatural, to be surprised by His mysteries. His wonder gives us power beyond our human strength, joy regardless of our circumstances, and, as the Apostle Paul wrote to the Ephesians, the ability to do *"exceedingly abundantly above all that we can ask, think, or imagine, according to the power that works in us"* (3:20).

God's Word is filled with numerous accounts of wonders that have occurred throughout history—from the beginning of creation, as recorded in the Book of Genesis, to the countless miraculous works of Jesus found in the four Gospels. As the Scriptures tell us, if all of His miracles, healings, and deliverances were written down, there would not be enough books to contain them! Then there are the Book of Acts, the Epistles, and the Book of Revelation, all of which are filled with the supernatural wonders of God performed by ordinary men and women like you and me.

Although I didn't see or experience anything miraculous, spectacular, or out of the ordinary immediately, that didn't prevent me from becoming more aware and listening more intently. I knew that if He were speaking to me about restoring His wonder, it was for a reason. I felt that He had some amazing things for me to discover, and I didn't want to miss anything! Once again, this would be something I could anticipate in my journey ahead.

The Wonder of Creation

Slowing down to enjoy the beauty of our surroundings is another way our King teaches us to rest in Him. His desire is for us, His Bride, to become more aware of the different places, spaces, and circumstances that allow us to see Him in all of His splendor and majesty. He is all the wonder we will ever need.

What is so amazing is that the wonders of God are found everywhere we go and everywhere we look. If we look up, we can see billions of diamonds—stars—to gaze upon at night when the sky is painted black. Each of these stars sparkles and shines with its unique shape and size. Some have even been used throughout the Scriptures for a specific purpose in the redemptive plan of God. One example is the star that led the Wise Men to travel a great distance to bring gifts to Jesus after His birth.

God also gave us the sun for times and seasons to bring light, life, and warmth during the daytime hours. He created the moon as a lesser light at night to stabilize our climate and to regulate the ocean's tides. He gave us the planets in our solar system, positioning them precisely so that the Earth does not get too close nor too far from the sun.

He placed us on this spectacular planet to be our home. From ocean depths brimming with unique life forms to sandy shores surrounding the seven continents. From majestic mountains to shimmering rivers, lakes, and streams. From rambling country roads to dusty deserts and winding forest trails. If we took the time to reflect on the wonders of this vast planet we have been given the honor of stewarding, we would forever be grateful and never get bored. *Selah!*

Our heavenly Father has blessed us with so much beauty to behold, yet we often fail to stop and recognize all that He has created for our enjoyment. *"He has made everything beautiful in its time"* (Ecclesiastes 3:11a).

The Wonder of His Presence

Let's explore three aspects of God's presence—His omnipresence, His presence within us, and His manifest Presence.

As I pondered the definition of the word ***omnipresence*** —"present in all places at all times,"—I realized that God's wonders are found everywhere because *He* is everywhere! We experience His *omnipresence* best through our five senses. He can be *seen* in everything around us—from the joyful faces of children at play to the changing colors of leaves in the fall. He can be *heard* in the sound of birds chirping on a cool spring morning or a violinist playing a passionate love song. We sense His presence when we catch the *scent* of flowers in a garden or *taste* freshly baked bread. We *feel* His *touch* in a gentle breeze, the rays of sun on our skin, or a warm embrace from a loved one.

There are other locations where it seems that it would be less likely for Him to be present. These are places where the darkest sins are prevalent—abortion clinics, sex trafficking organizations, sites where satanic rituals are practiced, etc. Yet, I believe these very places are where the wonder of God's presence, love, and protection might be felt the most.

King David expressed it this way:

"Where could I go from Your Spirit?
Where could I run and hide from Your face?
If I go up to heaven, You're there. If I go down to
the realm of the dead, You're there too!
If I fly with wings into the shining dawn, You're
there! If I fly into the radiant sunset, You're there
waiting! ... It's impossible to disappear from You
or to ask the darkness to hide me,

*For Your presence is everywhere, bringing light
into my night!"*
~Psalm 139:7-9, TPT

It doesn't matter where we are or what we're doing, His presence is always with us, surrounding us with His goodness.

Then there is the wonder of **God's presence within us.** According to First Corinthians 3:16, we have become His inner sanctuary—the place where His Spirit makes His permanent home. In the Gospel of John, we read that those who are in Christ have the presence of Holy Spirit dwelling within to be our Helper, the One who guides us into all truth (see 14:16).

His presence in us gives comfort when our hearts are breaking, encourages us in times of discouragement, counsels us when we need direction, and teaches us how to live according to God's Word. He strengthens us when we are weak, intercedes for us when we cannot pray, and empowers us to overcome any obstacles that come our way. With His presence abiding in us, we are more than conquerors.

This is a marvelous mystery! That the Spirit of the Living, Holy God, who created the universe, dwells inside us is more than we can comprehend!

Lastly, we experience the wonder of **God's manifest Presence.** To *manifest* is to "reveal, make known, make evident by showing or displaying something." There are times when God reveals His glory through a personal encounter with Him. These encounters can come when we are least expecting them. Often, they come during our times of praise and adoration. His Word says that He inhabits the praises of His people (see Psalm 22:3). Or they may come during times of prayer or reading the Scriptures when, by His Spirit, He causes a word or verse to leap off the page in confirmation of something He has spoken to our heart.

God's manifest Presence often comes during corporate worship and prayer. In the Book of Acts, those believers who were gathered in the Upper Room were all of one accord. Suddenly, the place was shaken by a rushing, mighty wind, and they were all filled with the Holy Spirit (see 2:1). It doesn't matter if it's the Upper Room or the living room; the church house or the prayer house. When His sons and daughters come together as one, His manifest Presence will show up, and lives will be changed for His glory.

Again, the wonder of His manifest Presence can come at any time or place—while driving in your vehicle, listening to music, watching a movie, reading a book, or going for a walk. I have experienced this numerous times throughout my years as a Christian.

Our Bridegroom King loves to surprise us with a manifest appearance. He does this when He chooses and how He chooses. He asks only that we prepare our hearts and make ourselves available to Him.

"*You Ravish My Heart!*"

As the second week of my journey came to an end, I sensed a change within myself. I felt more comfortable being alone—just me and Jesus. I felt much more settled than in the beginning. I was exercising more than before, walking at least five miles a day. I was taking naps during the day, too, which I had seldom done in the past. This was necessary to maintain my physical well-being while living a lifestyle of God's faith-rest.

My love for the Word of God had increased also. I became more focused as I read and meditated on certain words and subjects. One, in particular, was the word *ravish,* found in the Book of Song of Songs. This word had so touched my heart. I loved reading it in different translations, especially The Passion Translation. I found myself weeping throughout the day as I sat with my Beloved and allowed Him to take me (by His Spirit) deeper into His heart: *"Thou [Peggy] hast ravished my heart, my sister, my spouse; Thou hast ravished my heart with one of thine eyes, with one chain of thy neck"(Song of Songs 4:9, KJV,* author insertion).

To *ravish* is "to seize and carry off by force; to fill with intense delight; to fill with pleasure, joy, or happiness; to be overcome with intense feelings."

When we read verses like the one above, we associate them with words that we ourselves would speak over our Beloved King—and rightly so. He does ravish us —"overcome our hearts with intense feelings." However, on this particular day, I realized, from meditating on this verse, that *I* ravish *His* heart! That's right! With one glance of my eye—the eye of my heart—*I* captivate *Him.* When I gaze upon Him with a heart of love for Him, He turns His eyes—or heart of affection—toward me. It is then that He pours the liquid love of His presence—love that feels tangible—upon me.

Oh, that we would grasp how much our Beloved King longs to capture our gaze. We would forever be changed!

You Are So Beautiful!"

While waiting in silence one morning with my Beloved, I heard Him speak to my heart the word *"Beautiful!"* To possess beauty is "to have qualities that give great pleasure, excellence, or satisfaction to see, hear, or think about."

"Every part of you is beautiful, my darling.
Perfect is your beauty without flaw within."
~Song of Songs 4:7, TPT

As I read and reread this verse, I was ravished by the manifest Presence and love of my Beloved. It was as if He would not allow me to take my eyes off those words. I began to weep as I felt that every word was being planted —like a seed of revelation—deep within my heart and then bursting into bloom like a beautiful flower garden.

As His love for me unfolded, I heard Him say, *"I see you, my Bride, as beautiful. Even in the areas of your soul that haven't come into alignment with what I say about you in My Word, I still see you as so beautiful, Peggy."*

My response to Him came from the deepest part of my heart:

"Jesus, it amazes me when You whisper how much You love and adore me. This longing I feel for You is so overwhelming that it takes my breath away! I can't stop weeping as Your manifest Presence continues to brood over me even now. I want to savor this moment, every moment that I have with You, as a priceless treasure. I am so captivated by You and Your amazing love for me. Thank You for awakening my heart with Your words of life. Thank You for the freedom I am beginning to experience as I lean into Your rest. I have great expectations as I wait to see and experience Your wonders while on this journey. I can feel a bubbling up of joy as I anticipate what You have planned

for the two of us in the days ahead. You have captured my heart, and I am in awe of You, my Beloved Bridegroom King."

CHAPTER 7

Quietness: Be Still and Know

"My heart, O God, is quiet and confident.
Now I can sing with passion Your wonderful praises!"

~Psalm 57:7, TPT

The third week, I found myself navigating new territory once again. I had never studied quietness or even considered it as a lifestyle, so I knew this would be a challenging week. Regardless, I was determined to move forward and give it my all.

I invite you to join me as we discover together what quietness is all about. Maybe you can find some alone time to put some of the concepts the Lord gave me into practice for yourself. Maybe carve out a few hours or even a day or two and take a silent mini-retreat. You'll be surprised how much it will help when you incorporate this practice into your daily routine.

What Is Quietness?

Upon entering the third week of the journey with my Beloved, I began to recognize that He was leading me into greater depths of understanding of what it means to live a lifestyle according to Isaiah 30:15: *"In returning and rest you shall be saved; In quietness and trust shall be your strength."* For this to become a reality in my life, I would have to learn how to walk it out with my Beloved first.

Let's take a moment to examine this powerful Scripture and define the term *quietness*. In Hebrew, the word has different meanings, depending upon the verse of Scripture in which it is found. In this verse, the word is *Shaqat,* which means: "to be quiet, tranquil, at peace, rest, to keep silent, calm, lie still, settle, and be undisturbed." As I looked at each of these words, I thought, *Oh, wow! This is a lot, Lord! Am I going to be able to do this? I'm feeling a little overwhelmed right now.* Then, immediately, I felt an inner calm, and my thoughts began to quiet down.

Below is the definition of each word, with my thoughts following:

- **Tranquil:** "free from disturbance, calm" *(Not quite there yet.)*

- **Peace:** "completeness, soundness, harmony, wholeness, welfare" *(Getting there.)*

- **Rest:** "to be at peace with God, being silent, to stop, to cease, to relax, physical and spiritual rejuvenation" (*Yes! Mastered this one after the first two weeks!)*

- **Silent:** "to enter a sacred place within yourself" *(Is this even possible?)*

74

- **Quiet:** "a restful silence of soul, little or no motion, activity, or noise" *(Ugh! Got a long way to go with this one!)*

- **Calm:** "quietness, a settling of the mind" *(Better, but not there yet.)*

- **Still:** "to sink down, relax, let go of, to keep silence, to release" *(Much better at this!)*

- **Settled:** "bring to rest, establish, secure" *(Not sure yet.)*

- **Undisturbed:** "peaceful, serene, tranquil, unmoved, untouched" *(Maybe peaceful ... but the rest? Not even close!)*

I knew that to gain a deeper understanding of how to incorporate quietness into my daily life, I would have to meditate on the meaning of each word in the definition and then put it into practice when the opportunity arose. That would mean learning what it's like to quiet my spirit, mind, soul, and body. For this to happen, I would need to isolate myself as much as possible from all the distractions around me.

Do Not Disturb!

From that day forward, I decided it would be best to shut out the chatter from phone calls and remove the distractions that had previously hindered me by putting my phone in the "DO NOT DISTURB" mode. I did this for extended periods throughout my day, making it a point not to talk to anyone on the phone or in person unless absolutely necessary.

You might be thinking, *"What's wrong with having phone conversations or visiting people?"* Nothing. Except when you're called to a season of pulling away to be with Jesus. Engaging in conversations that are not fruitful or that take you away from your time with Him can be considered a distraction. This is especially true if you desire to give Him your full attention by staying focused on worship, prayer, and meditating on His Word. This had to become my top priority if I was going to gain a better understanding of quietness.

According to Psalm 46:10, we are instructed to *"Be still and know that He is God."* In this verse, the word *still* is "to let go, forsake, be feeble, and weak." In other words, we must let go or abandon what we normally accomplish in our own strength, humble ourselves, and fully depend on God. We become weak in our ability so that our Beloved King can show Himself strong in and through us.

To fully comprehend the value of *being still,* we must understand what it means *to know that He is God.* The word *know* in this verse is "to recognize, understand, have, be respected, be made aware, and have intimacy." *Intimacy*, in this context, is to have a personal, heart-to-heart, one-on-one relationship with the One who loves us and gave Himself for us.

As I've stated in a previous chapter, intimacy or knowing Jesus is developed through trust, and trust comes from spending time with Him. It's easier to trust someone when you know that person well, and once a relationship is developed, *being still* is also much easier to accomplish. I would come to understand this better in this week of quietness.

Becoming Quiet

Each day brought new lessons to be learned. My days became more routine. Waking up, making coffee, waiting to hear from my Beloved, spending quiet time with Him, and going for walks. Even though this initially felt mundane, I knew He was using it to teach me how to let go, rest, and give myself entirely to Him.

With the weather turning colder and being tucked away in the woods alone with no one to talk to, I found myself drawing even closer to the heart of my Beloved. I desired to hear the things He wanted to share with me. Each morning, He continued to speak to me by giving me a specific word and Scripture to study and meditate on. Even though this routine felt somewhat monotonous, I knew my Beloved was teaching me to value my time with Him and to spend it wisely.

The Scriptures tell us: *"Be diligent to present yourself approved to God, a worker who does not need to be ashamed, rightly dividing the word of truth"* (2 Timothy 2:15).

When we take the time to study and meditate on the Scriptures, the revelation from the seeds of God's Word is planted in our hearts and minds. This brings forth our spiritual growth and transformation.

Strangely, most of the words given to me each day by my Beloved did not seem to align with what I felt was necessary to gain a deeper understanding of *quietness.* Regardless, I was determined to follow His guidance instead of leaning on what I thought or felt. After all, He knows what is best for me and what lies ahead.

Be Steadfast

I explored the word *steadfast.* The Scripture verse: *"Therefore, my brothers and sisters, be steadfast, immovable* (not able to be moved), *always abounding* (excelling) *in the work of the Lord* (always doing your best and more than is needed) *being continually aware that your labor in the Lord is not futile nor wasted* (never without purpose)" (1 Corinthians 15:58, AMP).

To be *steadfast,* according to this verse, is "to be firmly fixed in place and firm in our belief." We must have a strong, confident understanding of who we are in Christ Jesus and a firm foundation in what we believe about who He is, according to the Scriptures. This is of great importance if we are going to walk in the authority given to us by our heavenly Father—as kings and priests here on earth (see Revelation 5:10).

When circumstances come to steal our joy or take us down a path that can lead us off course, being steadfast keeps us moving forward even when we feel like giving up. It also gives us the confidence and courage needed to accomplish what God has called us to do.

Pray with Me:

"Jesus, help me to be steadfast in every situation I face. I want to be confident and courageous when the giants of life come my way. Give me Your eyes to see and Your ears to hear when I'm up against things I don't understand or know how to approach. Give me heaven's perspective. I pray for the spirit of wisdom and revelation in the knowledge of You. I ask that the eyes of my understanding would be enlightened so that I

may know what You are calling me to. Thank You, Jesus, for hearing my prayer and answering according to Your will and purpose for my life. Amen!"

The Lord Is My Strength

Then, I was given the word *strength,* along with the Scripture: *"The LORD is my light and my salvation; whom shall, I fear? The LORD is the strength of my life; of whom shall I be afraid?"* (Psalm 27:1).

Psalm 27 is one of my favorites. The first verse alone is filled with such revelation. This psalm was King David's declaration of faith in God and who He is, especially in times of trouble. Although I will not go in depth regarding this chapter or verse here, I encourage you to study it for yourself. You will be richly blessed

I do want to focus on the word *strength* in verse 1. This word means "a fortified place, a defense, a fortress, a rock, a stronghold." A *fortified place* provides protection against an attack. A *fortress, a rock, and a stronghold* are also considered places of defense and protection. Each of these words and their meanings is encompassed in this one word, *strength.*

So, when the circumstances of life and the enemy of our souls bring fear and doubt, we can declare this Scripture, stand in faith, and know that our Lord is our fortified place, our fortress, and a place of defense against our enemies. Isn't that amazing? What wonderful protection our heavenly Father has given those who belong to Him. *"God is our refuge and strength, a very present help in trouble"* (Psalm 46:1).

A Kiss from My Beloved

As my day came to an end, I felt drawn by my Beloved to spend the evening with Him, reading chapters 4-6 in the Song of Songs, the Passion Translation of the Bible. As soon as I began reading Chapter 4, my eyes brimmed with tears. Verse 2 touched my heart in such a deep, profound way. *"When I look at you, I see how you have taken My fruit and tasted My Word. Your life has become clean and pure, like a lamb washed and newly shorn. You show grace and balance with truth on display."*

Such life-giving words spoken over me through this verse. *Oh, how beautiful!* I pondered. *My Beloved sees me! He knows my desire to be obedient to follow Him at all costs.*

This brought me such encouragement. Just one verse helped me see how much it pleases Him when His beloved Bride takes the time to feast on His Word. The spiritual growth that takes place in us when we do so is priceless.

I continued to read the three chapters very slowly—as if they were precious water to quench my thirst after a day of wandering in the desert. It felt as if my heart would explode with joy from His passionate love and presence. Each word seemed to be more alive than ever before. My heart devoured the words, written like a love letter from a long-lost lover. I couldn't stop weeping. "Jesus, You've captured my heart in a new and profound way through Your life-giving Word."

As I continued to read, my Beloved had me pause at Song of Songs 6 and read three verses over and over. It felt as if He was speaking the words personally and directly to me. I could sense them ministering healing to my soul, reminding me once again that I am His and His passionate desire is for me, His Bride.

The Word of God comes alive even more when we make it personal. Try reading the verses below as a love letter from our King to you, inserting your name where my name appears:

My Beloved said: *"I can't resist the passion of these eyes that I adore, Peggy. Overpowered by a glance, My ravished heart—undone. Held captive by your love, I am truly overcome! For your undying devotion to me, Peggy, is the most yielded sacrifice ... I could have chosen any from among the vast multitude of royal ones who follow me. But you, Peggy, are unique, unrivaled in beauty, without equal, beyond compare, the perfect one, the favorite one"* (Song of Songs 6:5, 8-9, author paraphrase).

Selah!

Let's Pray Together:

"Holy Spirit, increase my hunger to know Jesus in a deeper, more profound way. I want to be so thirsty for Him that nothing else apart from Him satisfies. Just as the Apostle Paul prayed, I pray also: 'I kneel humbly in awe before the Father of our Lord Jesus, the Messiah, the perfect Father of every father and child in heaven and on the earth. And I pray, Father, that You would unveil within me the unlimited riches of Your glory and favor until supernatural strength floods my innermost being with Your divine might and explosive power'" (Ephesians 3:14-16, TPT).

Obedience—Better than Sacrifice

I felt extra refreshed and rested after the beautiful evening of heart-to-heart intimacy with my King. In fact, I slept much longer than I normally do, as I was there to get physical as well as spiritual rest. Plus, I had extra time to sleep longer and even take naps if I chose to.

When I was fully awake, I got out of bed, prepared my coffee, and planted myself in the recliner. I sat there quietly, waiting to hear from my Beloved. He wasn't in a hurry to speak to me that morning, so I sat still and listened. As I leaned in with my spiritual ears to hear, He whispered the word, *"Obedience."*

"What Scripture would You have me meditate on, Lord?" I asked.

Still listening intently, I heard these two verses:

"Has the Lord as great a delight in burnt offerings and sacrifices as He does in obedience to the voice of the Lord? Behold, to obey is better than sacrifice and to heed is better than the fat of rams" (1 Samuel 15:22), followed by Isaiah 1:19: *"If you are willing and obedient, you shall eat the best of the land"* (AMP).

The word *obedience* means "discipline, hearing, submission, giving attention to, and submissiveness." Obedience is a key discipline to receiving God's best for us. When we obey what He asks us to do, we grow in maturity, and our lives will produce fruit.

I'm sure you're probably aware that when given a word like *obedience,* most likely there will be a test to see what is in our heart concerning that concept. So, it should come as no surprise that I was tested very soon after that.

The Test

After spending time with Jesus, I decided to listen in on a prayer conference call that I normally lead. It was good to hear other people praying and to learn how much I had been missed.

When someone on the call expressed a particular need, I rushed to offer a prayer. Surely the Lord wouldn't mind if I prayed for just one person. After all, this was one of His children!

The prayer call ended, and I reached for a jacket as I headed outside to enjoy the crisp morning air with my Beloved. As we were walking, I felt a gentle pay-attention nudge in my spirit concerning the prayer call I had participated in earlier.

Then I heard Him say, *"Remember the word I spoke to you first thing this morning?"*

"Yes, it was *obedience.*"

"Did you join that call and pray for that person because I asked you to or because you wanted to? Just what was your motive for praying for that person?"

I thought for a moment before confessing, "I did it out of my own desire and not because You asked me to, Lord. Honestly, I joined the call because I missed praying and hearing others pray."

Suddenly, an overwhelming sense of grief washed over my heart as I realized that I had disobeyed my Beloved. He had asked me not to join in on any prayer calls unless He prompted me.

My Beloved knew what I was feeling and corrected me gently: *"Peggy, I desire to teach you to wait on Me and listen for My voice. I want you to learn how to walk with Me and not be led by your own desires or what others expect of you. If you do this, you will prosper, and your life will bring forth abundant fruit."*

"Jesus, You are right as always. I ask for Your forgiveness for my disobedience."

"Of course I forgive you, and I will still bless what you did because your heart was in the right place. But remember, obedience is greater than sacrifice." (Or, "Obeying the Lord is

better than doing what *you* think is the right thing to do!" (Peggy's paraphrase).

After my heart-to-heart with my Beloved, I continued my walk in silence for a bit longer, thinking about our conversation and how essential it is to obey, even though at times it might not make sense to us. As we honor God with our obedience, He honors us for our sacrifice.

As we were finishing our walk, I prayed, "Jesus, thank You for being so loving and kind. Thank You for what you are teaching me on this journey. As I ponder all that You have been showing me while I've been here, I sense You are calling me to something greater—something beyond myself. I feel it is Your plan for me to teach the concept of daily walking in the Isaiah 30:15 Returning, Rest, Quietness, and Confidence journey. If this is true, give me greater insight into what this would mean so that I can help others."

I didn't get an immediate response, but I knew He had heard me, He always hears me. I could feel His presence, and I know He will reveal more in His timing.

Our Beloved King has a purpose for each of us. He longs for us to be connected to His heart and to listen for His voice when He calls us to draw near. His desire is for daily intimacy with us. What an honor and privilege that He, the King of the Universe, wants to spend time with us. Out of all of God's creation, we are most valued and blessed to have this privilege.

As you read the following verses, allow them to draw you to the heart of our King:

"The one I love calls to me:
Arise, my dearest. Hurry, my darling.
Come away with me!
I have come as you have asked to draw you to my
heart and lead you out.
For now is the time, my beautiful one.
"The season has changed, the bondage of your
barren winter has ended, and the season of hiding is
over and gone.
The rains have soaked the earth and left it bright
with blossoming flowers.
The season for singing and pruning the vines has
arrived. I hear the cooing of doves in our land, filling
the air with songs
To awaken you and guide you forth.
"Can you not discern this new day of destiny
breaking forth around you?
The early signs of my purposes and plans are
bursting forth. The budding vines of new life are now
blooming everywhere.
The fragrance of their flowers whispers, "There is
change in the air."
Arise, my love, my beautiful companion,
and run with me to the higher place.
For now is the time to arise
and come away with Me."

~ Song of Songs 2:10-13, TPT

Lead Me

With each new day, I felt closer to the heart of my King. I sensed His nearness throughout my day. From the moment I woke up, I was given another word, phrase, song, and Scripture to carry with me throughout my day. I became comfortable with the quietness. The distractions were gone, and I began to hear the voice of my Beloved in different ways. Usually, I heard Him speak to my heart or thoughts. Now I was picking up the languages of knowing, sensing, and perceiving. I could feel that my spiritual understanding had heightened. I knew this was necessary for a new level of growth and maturity.

One morning, I heard the word *lead,* and I was directed by Holy Spirit to read and meditate on Psalm 23, specifically verse 2:

> *"He makes me lie down in green pastures;*
> *He **leads** me beside the still waters."*

To lead is "to guide, as to a watering place; to bring to a place of rest; to refresh."

Take a moment to speak this verse out loud to the Lord as an offering of thanksgiving to Him. "Lord Jesus, I thank You for making me lie down in green pastures. Thank You for leading me beside still waters so that You can restore my soul."

Now, take a few minutes to ponder this scene in your heart:

Picture yourself lying in a pasture of beautiful green grass with Jesus beside you. Take a deep breath as you feel the warmth of the sun beaming down on your face, consuming your entire being. Then picture Him taking you by the hand to lift you and lead you beside the gentle, still waters. Feel His rest. Let Him refresh you with His peace until you are completely immersed in it.

Sweet Surprise

It was later than usual when I started out for my afternoon walk. In this month of January, it was getting dark much earlier. I normally began my walk at around four o'clock in the afternoon, but that day it was closer to five.

While walking the trail I normally take, I happened to look to my right and spot an open, grassy field through the woods. *I haven't seen that place before,* I marveled. *I've been walking this trail every day for the past two weeks, and I have never noticed this.*

Before my discovery, I had been thinking about the word *lead* and realized I hadn't felt or seen anything significant all day. Then, suddenly, the Lord surprised me with a grassy field on my walk through the woods.

With mounting excitement, I peeked through the trees to see if I could find a way to get to that place. If the Lord has brought me this far, He surely means for me to go there. *Maybe the side road at the beginning of the trail that I've been passing by every day will lead me down to the field,* I was thinking.

Since it was nearly dusk, and I had no idea how far I would have to walk, I decided to wait and go the next day. As I walked past the road at the top of the hill, Holy Spirit prompted me to turn around. "But, Lord, it's getting late," I protested. "I don't know how far I'll have to walk." Then Holy Spirit reminded me of my word, *lead,* and Psalm 23:2: *"He makes me lie down in green pastures. He leads me beside still waters."*

Suddenly, it dawned on me that I must do this today. My mind raced. *Whatever I discover there will align with what He is speaking to me through today's word. Sometimes we must take a leap of faith and jump, or in this case, GO. He will protect me.*

So, eager to see what my Beloved had for me this time, I turned to the right and made my way down the road. A few minutes later, I found myself at my destination. To my surprise, there was not only a grassy, green field but also a flowing stream.

Overwhelmed by joy and excitement. I could hardly believe that my Beloved had given me the word *lead* and then waited until the end of the day to surprise me with this wonderful gift! He knows how much I love rivers and streams! Now I had a perfect place to spend time with Him in quietness surrounded by the beauty of creation.

Disappointing News

I received a phone call that night from my sister, Linda, informing me that our brother, Bobby, had been taken to the hospital and diagnosed with pneumonia and the COVID-19 virus. Upon checking him, they discovered that one of his lungs was filled with fluid. She said he was having breathing issues and might have to be placed on a ventilator. I thanked her for contacting me, asked her to keep me updated on any changes, and assured her that I would be praying.

After ending our conversation, I remembered that, at different times throughout the day, I had gone into fervent intercessory prayer. I would weep as I felt Holy Spirit groaning deep within me. I kept sensing it was for one of my family members, but I didn't know who or what it was about. This is why we should stay alert and posture ourselves to *"pray without ceasing."*

As this week of quietness ended, I had more clarity as to why my Beloved had given me words and Scriptures that didn't seem to fit with the week's theme. He knew I would need them to give me strength and help me to fully trust Him for what I couldn't see. As you will discover in the next chapter, they became an anchor I would need for the trial ahead, and I prayed:

> *"Jesus, thank You for Your creation and the beautiful place You blessed me with. It's like a*

secret hideaway just for the two of us. I look forward to our time together there.

Lord, I want to bring my brother before You. I trust that You are his Healer. Nothing is impossible with You. Take this situation that seems hopeless and turn it for Your good. May You receive all glory and honor. from what seems to be a hopeless situation. Cover him with Your precious blood. Protect and heal him. I also ask that you comfort my mom and the rest of my family. Strengthen their faith in You and help them to trust in You. I ask this in Your name, Jesus. Amen. "

CHAPTER 8
Trust in the Lord

"Trust in the LORD with all your heart,
And do not lean on your own understanding.
In all your ways acknowledge Him,
And He will direct your paths."

~Proverbs 3:5-6

T he next few days would present one of the toughest challenges I had yet faced—trusting God when things seem hopeless. In this case, it was my brother's serious battle with the COVID-19 virus. Trusting requires faith to believe in something or someone we don't fully understand or haven't seen.

The key Scripture for this chapter—Proverbs 3:5-6—instructs us to trust in the Lord with all our hearts, even when our minds and our circumstances are telling us otherwise. The word *trust* in this passage is "to rely on, to put confidence in, or to secure." This kind of trust comes from taking the necessary time to cultivate an intimate relationship with God, our Father; Jesus, His Son, and Holy Spirit, as I have emphasized throughout this book. When we trust Him, we are not to depend on our human understanding. Instead, we are to push past what we think we know, or how we perceive a situation, and ask Holy Spirit to help us see from His perspective—the perspective that comes through God's Word.

Next, we are asked to acknowledge Him in every situation we encounter and in everything that pertains to our daily lives. We are to recognize Him and make decisions with His help. This isn't always easy. Sounds good when we read or speak these words, but it's quite different when we are head on with the reality of living it out. But when we obey, He has promised to guide us in the right direction.

"Delight in Me"

As I sat with my Beloved extra-early in the morning, I was not asking Him any questions or even requesting healing for my sick brother. I only wanted to wait for Him to speak. In the past, when difficulties arose, I would immediately begin suggesting *my* solutions to the problem. Today, I just wanted to be with Him. I wanted to draw close to His heart and hear what *He* had to say.

As I leaned in to listen, He softly whispered, *"Delight yourself in Me."* I knew this was an invitation to press in and pay attention to what He wanted to show me. I then heard the rest of that Scripture verse: *"... and He will give you the desires of your heart"* (Psalm 37:4).

To *delight* is from the root word meaning "pleasure and enjoyment." So, if we find pleasure and enjoyment in the

Lord, His Word assures us that He will give us the "desires" ("petitions") of our hearts. Of course, this refers to those whose desires are in alignment with His. Many will quote the second part of that verse, forgetting that the promise comes with a condition.

While meditating on this verse, I realized that it doesn't say anything about the Lord having to delight in *me!* Then I thought, *He doesn't have to be asked to delight in you and me because He delights in us always. Jesus finds so much pleasure and enjoyment in us that He gave His life as a sacrifice just to draw us to Himself forever.*

The Prophet Isaiah reminds us how much the Father delights in His Son: *"My Servant whom I uphold; my Chosen One in whom My soul delights"* (42:1, AMP).

"Jesus, I desire to find true pleasure and enjoyment in You. I want to be in alignment with Your desires in every area of my life and to bring pleasure and enjoyment to You. I know You gave me the word **delight** *to meditate on for a specific reason. Lord, I choose to do my best to make it a lifestyle to daily delight in You. Right now, the number-one desire of my heart is for Bobby to be healed ... Is that Your plan for him as well?"*

Although I didn't get an answer to my question, I chose to remain in faith and to trust that my Beloved is working all things together for good.

Crisis Call

While finishing a late breakfast, I received a phone call from my sister Laura. I was anticipating a good report. After all, it had not been long since I had presented my request to my Beloved.

But Laura was crying. Not wanting to expect the worst, I remained calm. "What's wrong, Laura? What's going on?"

"Bobby went into cardiac arrest this morning! They were able to revive him, but the doctor said it doesn't look good. They are having to transport him to a larger hospital where there is more advanced equipment for his level of care," she replied through her tears.

I took a deep breath. "Well, transferring him to a larger facility is a good thing. Let's just trust God and keep praying. And please keep me posted."

She agreed, and when we hung up, all I could do was turn to my Beloved who knows all things:

"Lord, it's not easy being so far from my family when my brother is in critical condition in the hospital. Jesus, I have prayed, declared Your Word, and reached out to others to pray for Bobby. Your Word says, 'You're the God who heals ... and nothing is impossible with You.' Lord, I believe it's Your desire to heal my brother. I thank You for hearing my request and answering according to Your will. In Your Name, Jesus, I pray. Amen."

I can't explain the level of peace I was feeling at that moment, even though deep in my heart, I knew that my brother might not survive this crisis. I was doing my best to have faith regardless of how hopeless the situation appeared. I chose to stay in the place of peace and believe God for His best for Bobby.

When we place our trust in Jesus, who is the Prince of Peace, His peace wraps around us like a warm blanket on a chilly day. It's like being in a peace bubble! Nothing can touch us because not only are we inside of peace, but peace is inside of us!

Jesus said, *"Peace I leave with you. My peace I give to you; not as the world gives do I give to you. Let not your heart be troubled, neither let it be afraid"* (John 14:27).

By afternoon, the temperature had warmed up, so I decided to walk to the river. It felt so good to be outside in the warm, sunny air. The sound of the water rushing over the rocks calmed my spirit.-But I was soon to learn that it was only the calm before the storm.

Around four o'clock, I was sitting on the riverbank, listening to the music of the river and reading my Bible, when I received a call from my sister Linda. She was sobbing. "Peggy, we're on our way to the hospital. Bobby has had another cardiac arrest after being transferred to the larger facility. The doctor says he doesn't have much time. He's calling for the family."

I could hear my other three sisters crying in the background. Trying my best to hold it together, I replied, "Remember, God is greater than anything the doctors have to say. We must continue to trust Him. Let me know as soon as you arrive at the hospital." I prayed with them, then ended the call.

After talking with my sisters, I asked Jesus, "Do I need to leave now to drive to North Carolina to be with my family, or should I wait until tomorrow?" I listened for His answer. *"Tomorrow,"* was the answer I heard in my spirit.

Even after that sobering update from Linda, I was still experiencing so much peace. *This must be the kind of peace Jesus felt when He received the news that His friend Lazarus was near death,* I thought to myself. I recalled the familiar biblical account when Jesus waited four days before traveling to Bethany because He knew that He would raise Lazarus from the dead.

Gathering my journal and Bible, I left the riverbank to walk and pray. In my spirit, I heard this verse: *"This sickness is not unto death, but for the glory of God, that the Son of God may be glorified through it"* (John 11:4).

My heart leapt. "Lord," I spoke out loud, "does this mean that Bobby is going to have a resurrection experience? That would be amazing! It would give everyone the opportunity to see Your miraculous power at work. Please, Lord, let it be so!"

I waited for His answer, but I didn't hear anything. Only silence. I thought it strange that my Beloved would give me that verse and yet not answer my question. However, I have come to understand that His ways are higher than my ways, so I would continue to trust Him even though I didn't get my answer right away.

Back at the cottage, I received another call from my sister Laura. As I heard her broken sobs, I braced myself. "Bobby didn't make it." She could barely utter the words. "He's gone, Peggy! He's in heaven now."

For a moment, it felt that time stood still. I could hear my sisters weeping in the background, but I couldn't say anything. I don't know if I was in shock or disbelief. Even in that moment, though, I was sensing so much peace. I'm normally the stronger one among my siblings, but to feel this kind of peace at the passing of our brother was remarkable! Finally, I was able to ask, "What happened?"

Laura proceeded to fill me in. "His organs shut down, and he was just too weak to fight anymore."

On my sisters' drive back home from the hospital, I listened to their conversation and prayed for comfort and strength for all of us. I let them know that I would be leaving South Carolina the next morning to join the family. "I love you and we'll get through this together … with God's help," I assured them before ending the call.

Resting on the sofa. I reflected on all that had happened over the past couple of days—every detail. It felt surreal. Yet, I was still bathed in supernatural peace. After a while, my mind clicked into gear. I should call my son and daughter, Devin and Samantha, who were close to their uncle. This news would be difficult for them—the most difficult since the passing of my dad in 1993. I tried to reach my mom, but she wasn't answering her phone. And then there were all those who had prayed for my brother. I must let them know the news and ask for prayer for my family in the days ahead.

In response to my texts, I received many phone calls from spiritual leaders and friends. Their words of sympathy and support encouraged me. But as usual, I turned to my Beloved for the strength that only He can provide:

"Father, it's difficult to believe this happened so quickly! My brother was admitted to the hospital on Thursday, and only two days later, he is no longer with us! Father, my heart aches for my mom. She doesn't have strong faith and often keeps her feelings inside instead of expressing them. We were supposed to be celebrating her 81st birthday soon. How will she get through this?

I am also concerned for my sister-in-law, Frankie, and their son and daughter. And then there are my siblings and my nieces and nephews. We are a large, close-knit family, and I feel this loss is going to shake us all tremendously. As our

100

loving heavenly Father, I ask for Your strength and comfort for all of us. Thank You, Father." In Jesus' name. Amen."

Joy and Peace in the Pain

With the four-hour drive to North Carolina ahead of me, I woke up early to spend time with my Beloved. As I sat quietly, waiting to hear from Him, He spoke the word *joy* to my spirit, and this Scripture from the Book of Nehemiah came to mind: *"Do not grieve, for the joy of the LORD is your strength"* (8:10).

Pondering this Scripture and the word *joy,* I said, "It's not that I don't trust You, Jesus, but I'm confused. Today of all days, why would You give me this word? It seems so inappropriate for the occasion. With the passing of my brother, how can I have joy? Even though I'm experiencing great peace, I wouldn't say I'm joyful. So, Lord, I need some help in understanding."

I did some study of the Hebrew meaning of this word, specifically in this verse of Scripture. According to Strong's *Concordance of the Bible,* this is the only verse in the Old Testament Scriptures where the word *joy* has a one-word meaning—"gladness." The word *gladness* means "experiencing joy, pleasure, and rejoicing."

In the New Testament—Galatians 5:22—the word *joy,* sandwiched between *love* and *peace,* is considered one of the nine fruits of the Spirit. In this verse, *joy* has multiple meanings—"rejoicing, happiness, gladness, joyfulness, and rejoice greatly."

After studying *joy,* I was still confused as to why *this* word and why *now,* of all times! Then it struck me! Any joy I feel is fueled by God's love, which brings peace even when my life is in chaos. I was beginning to see that it's not *my* joy, but "the joy of the Lord" *in me* that will give me strength when I need it most. As difficult as the days ahead might be, I am comforted to know that *His* strength will be *my* strength.

A *"Precious"* Death

At 6:45 the next morning, I packed my car and left my cozy abode in the woods to make the trip to North Carolina. I could feel my Beloved giving me strength as I drove. The peace I continued to feel was unexplainable in the natural. It felt like a combination of *"the peace that passes understanding"* (Philippians 4:7) and *"perfect peace"* (Isaiah 26:3) given when our minds are fixed on Him because we trust in Him. When we trust the Lord in the difficult times as well as the times when we can't see clearly, His perfect peace floods our hearts and minds.

Once again, I found myself wondering why I was given the Scripture from John 11:4 regarding this sickness not being unto death, but for the glory of God. *"Why would You give me that verse, Lord, and then allow my brother to die? It just doesn't make sense. But although I don't understand, I'm trusting You to give me clarity at the right time."*

On the road, I reflected on Bobby's life. He was five years younger than I and the twin of my sister, Donna. Growing up, they were polar opposites. Bobby was the quieter of the two, but as he grew older, he developed a more outgoing personality. He never met a stranger and could carry on a conversation with anyone. Everybody knew who he was in our area. With his great sense of humor, he kept us laughing, so there was never a dull moment at family gatherings.

More importantly, Bobby was gentle and kind and would give you the shirt off his back, but he could also speak his mind when necessary. After our dad passed, it was as if Bobby took Dad's place as protector of the family, especially his sisters. We could call on him at any time, and he would be there to help. I was so honored to call him my brother. I would miss him terribly.

Together Again

When I arrived at my destination, I was running a bit late for the Sunday worship service and went directly to the church where our brother Mark was pastor. Walking from the parking lot, I prayed, *"Thank You, Holy Spirit, for Your presence with me. Please give me the strength to encourage my family and continue to keep me in Your perfect peace so that I can speak words of life. I'm trusting You, Lord, to help us in this time of loss. I know You are with us."*

The service had already started, so I slipped into a seat beside some of my family members. I could see the sadness on their faces and feel the pain of their broken hearts. Yet, even with tears flowing down the faces of many in the congregation, I remained calm and at peace.

Mark, too, struggled to contain his grief as he attempted to bring the message God had placed on his heart. He and Bobby had been particularly close, so I knew this was difficult for him.

Once the service was over, I was able to connect with the rest of my family. Tears flowed even more freely as we embraced, some of my siblings still questioning how this had happened so suddenly and unexpectedly. Before I could share my own questions, members of the congregation pressed in to express their condolences. I felt God's grace and love giving me a surge of strength I had not known before.

Making our way out of the church, we gathered at Mark's house. It was good to be together, even though one was missing. Being able to share funny stories, to laugh, cry, and reminisce about Bobby's life brought some joy and healing. The Scriptures tell us: *"A joyful heart is good medicine"* (Proverbs 17:22, NASB) and *"You keep track of all my sorrows. You have collected all my tears in Your bottle"* (Psalm 56:8, NLT). Laughter and tears! Bobby would have loved it! He was always the life of the party!

I found myself saying very little, just listening to the others as they shared. Not that I didn't have anything to say, because I did. However, being hidden away with my Beloved for uninterrupted periods of time had taught me to listen more and speak only when necessary. As an intercessor—one who feels the burdens of others and prays for them—during my quiet time and with the help of the Holy Spirit, I would be interceding for my family.

"Likewise, the Spirit also helps in our weaknesses. For we do not know what we should pray for as we ought, but the Spirit Himself makes intercession for us with groanings which cannot be uttered" (Romans 8:26).

As darkness fell, I suddenly felt exhausted. It was going to be a long, tiring week, and with my hotel another 45-minute drive down the road, I decided to leave and get some rest. I had felt the peace of the Lord all day, even during the most emotional times. However, as I drove away, it was as if the floodgates were lifted and the dam broke.

I wept and wept as my spirit began to intercede, joining the groanings of Holy Spirit. I cried so deeply I could hardly breathe. I thought I was going to have to pull over on the side of the road because I could barely see through my tears.

In about half an hour, my tearful intercession began to subside. Although tired, I continued in the "bubble of peace" I had experienced earlier, and I arrived safely at the hotel.

Before crawling into bed, I fell to my knees once more.

"Holy Spirit, thank You for Your comfort and peace. Continue to strengthen, comfort, and encourage my family. Give Frankie and others insight as they make the funeral arrangements. With the pandemic and all its rules and regulations, it will be difficult to plan the memorial service. Father, may Your loving arms wrap around my mom's heart as she grieves the loss of her son. I can't imagine that kind of pain! But as a loving Father, You understand only too well. In Your precious Name I pray. Amen."

CHAPTER 9

Confident in Trials

"We are confident, yes, well pleased rather to be absent from the body and to be present with the Lord."
—2 Corinthians 5:8

I lay in bed the next morning, replaying in my mind all that had transpired over the past few days since Bobby's passing. Then, out of nowhere, reality hit me: *My brother is no longer with us. This can't be real. It feels like a terrible dream, and I'm ready to wake up!*

However, it was not a dream. It was the raw, real truth.

Tears began to flow down my cheeks. Not tears of hopelessness, because I knew I would one day be with Bobby again. These were expressions of sorrow resulting from his absence. These were tears reminding me of how much I already missed him. No more family gatherings. No more phone calls. No more sending me comical messages and videos via text and FB Messenger. *I'm going to miss those tender "Bobby moments."*

I cried even more as I browsed through my cell phone, looking at pictures of my brother. The most recent ones were taken the past Christmas when we gathered at his home for

Christmas Eve brunch. You could see—from the huge grin on his face—how excited he was to play host that year. He reminded me so much of our daddy. Sometimes I would catch a glimpse of him and think that he *was* Daddy. Now they were both gone. *This doesn't seem fair. Why now?*

As I reflected on Bobby's life, I was reminded of how we often take for granted time spent with those we love, forgetting that none of us are promised tomorrow. We should do our best to cherish every moment together as if it were our last.

Even though my heart was aching, I was encouraged when Holy Spirit reminded me of this Scripture: *"But I do not want you to be ignorant, brethren, concerning those who have fallen asleep, lest you sorrow as others who have no hope. For if we believe that Jesus died and rose again, even so God will bring with Him those who sleep in Jesus"* (1 Thessalonians 4:13-14).

When Jesus gave His life for us on the cross, He defeated death through the power of His resurrection from the dead. This assures me that death is not the final destination for those who have given their hearts to Him. There is great comfort in knowing that I will see Bobby again—and all those who are in Christ.

"Abide in My Love"

After looking at pictures of my brother and reflecting on our abbreviated life together, I realized that I hadn't spent any quality time that morning with my Beloved. My family would be gathering later, so I knew if I was to have time alone with Him, it would need to be now.

As I had done each morning, I sat in bed, closed my eyes, and waited quietly until I felt His presence. When I whispered, "Speak, Lord, I'm listening," I heard Him say, *"Abide."* He then prompted me to read the Scripture verses in John 15, where He shares the value of abiding in Him.

To *abide* is "to stay, to remain, to live, and to dwell in." To abide in Christ, then, is to live a life of oneness in Him. It is to follow Him and His example of a lifestyle that is obedient to the will of the Father in all that we do and say.

As I read the verses in John 15, I was reminded of the importance of abiding in Jesus, the Vine, who continually sustains us. It doesn't matter what our circumstances are, we must stay connected to Him. He is our Life Source. Apart from Him, we can do nothing, but with Him, we can do all things (see John 15:5). This is true for all who believe and trust in Him as Lord and Savior.

I knew that each verse in John 15, with its deep revelation, could have a significant spiritual implication for me on my journey. However, I needed to know the specific verse my Beloved was speaking at this moment to help me in the days just ahead.

I slowly reread the verses, asking Holy Spirit to show me which one He wanted me to meditate on. Pausing at verse 9, I read: *"As the Father loved Me, I also have loved you; abide in My love."* Immediately, these four words jumped off the page: *"Abide in My love."*

I then felt prompted to read this verse in the Passion Translation of the Bible: *"I love each of you with the same love that the Father loves me. You must continually let my love nourish your heart."*

Tears filled my eyes as I read those beautiful words once again. It was difficult for me to comprehend that I'm loved by Jesus in the same way that the Father loves Him. Now the tears streamed down my face as His abiding presence filled my heart with a love I had not felt before. It's as if I were inside His love, and His love was nourishing my hurting heart.

At that moment, I felt my heavenly Father embrace me as only a loving father can do. Engulfed in His abiding presence, I began to weep as I released all that I was feeling in my soul. My Beloved Father whispered, *"My grace is sufficient for you, for My strength is made perfect in weakness"* (2 Corinthians 12:9).

I continued to remain with Him for a while longer. I envisioned myself like a child, sitting on His lap, with His loving arms around me. I could feel His sweet presence comforting me, healing my broken heart. This is exactly what

I needed to help me through my day so I could help others in their struggle. It was then that I was reminded of these verses from 2 Corinthians:

"Blessed be the God and Father of our Lord Jesus Christ, the Father of mercies and God of all comfort, who comforts us in all our tribulation, that we may be able to comfort those who are in any trouble, with the comfort with which we ourselves are comforted by God" (1:3-4).

When we take the time to sit with our heavenly Father, to be still and wait for Him, He will draw near and encourage us in His love. He knows what we need at every moment and in every situation.

I got out of bed and prepared for the day before picking up Devin, Samantha, and her girls. When we arrived, we met with the rest of the family at my brother Mark's house around lunchtime to select pictures for the funeral home to create a DVD for the memorial service.

This turned into an all-day get-together. We laughed and cried as we looked through the pictures and shared stories and memories of Bobby. We had plenty to eat, thanks to church members and friends stopping by to bring food. That's one of the great things about church families: they love to cook, they love to eat, and they love to share comfort food with those who are grieving the loss of loved ones.

In addition, there is great comfort in the closeness of family, so no one was in a hurry to leave. It's as if we were a lifeline for one another. We would need this for the days ahead.

"My Peace I Give You"

The next morning, I woke up feeling deeply rested and still experiencing a level of peace I can't explain. Even though I was aware of my own grief and the emotional stress of others in my family, I was at peace. He reminded me of what His Word says about peace in John's Gospel:

"Peace, I leave with you, My peace I give to you,
not as the world gives do I give to you.
Let not your heart be troubled, neither let it
be afraid."
~John 14:27

Anticipating that the next couple of days would probably be the most difficult, I sensed that I should take some time that morning to meditate on peace and to gain a better understanding of its meaning through God's Word.

The Greek meaning of *peace* is "harmony, tranquility, safety, welfare, health, lack of strife, and freedom from emotional worry and frustration."

This kind of peace is one of the nine fruits of the Holy Spirit found in Galatians 5:22-23a: *"But the fruit of the Spirit is love, joy, peace, longsuffering [or patience], kindness, goodness, faithfulness, gentleness, and self-control."*

These nine fruits are available to us as believers through the power of Holy Spirit who lives in us. I think we sometimes forget that the fruits are already in us because *He* is in us. If we find ourselves lacking in one of the fruits, we should ask Holy Spirit to help us increase in that area and remove any obstacles that would hinder the fruit—and in this case, peace—from growing in our lives.

With His peace, I don't have to be troubled or afraid.

The Viewing

At eleven o'clock, my family was scheduled to meet at the funeral home for the first viewing of Bobby's body. To me, this would be the most difficult day of the whole process—the part I dreaded most.

When hearing the news of the passing of a loved one, you experience the initial shock. *This can't be happening!* It's as if your mind keeps saying, *It's not real!* even though you've heard the news for yourself.

Then comes the viewing of the body. That's when reality strikes. You are no longer just hearing about it; now you are seeing it with your own eyes. Grief delivers a gut-punch, and you struggle to breathe. No one can prepare you for what you will experience. It's different for each person, depending upon their relationship with the individual who has passed. *Once again, I'm so thankful to have You to lean on, Jesus!*

I left the hotel at 10:00 to pick up Devin and Samantha. Since we have such a large family, the three of us planned to meet the others in the parking lot of the funeral home so we could walk in together. There wasn't much conversation, only sad faces and swollen eyes. I could tell that everyone was nervous and dreading this next step. I did my best to hug as many family members as possible, hoping to encourage them. Despite the pandemic that was in full sway, our family had chosen not to wear masks when together, so we were not hindered in expressing our love and grief.

We made our way inside and gathered in a large side room to receive instructions from the funeral home director and to pray together. Then we proceeded to the foyer and formed a line outside the sanctuary door.

My mom with her fiancé; Bobby's wife and their family; our brother Mark and his family entered the sanctuary first. A few minutes later, the rest of the siblings lined up according to age and followed them.

Up to this moment, I had felt so much peace, but now anxiety crept in. I began to speak the word *"Peace"* to myself softly. As I waited in line, I kept repeating, "Remain in peace, Peggy. Peace, peace, peace. He will keep you in perfect peace, so stay focused on Him."

I could hear the sobs of those in front of me as well as behind me as we slowly made our way toward the open casket. Devin was on my left side and Samantha on my right. As we neared the casket, I braced myself. Once my sister Linda and her family moved forward, we walked up to see Bobby's lifeless body lying there.

All at once, the reality of his death was more than I could bear, and I released a groan from deep within my soul that I could not contain. It was so strong that if Devin and Samantha had not been holding me up, I would have fallen to my knees.

I cried and cried as waves of pain and grief overcame me. I could feel the deep groan of the Spirit stirring within me. I walked to the back of the room, leaned against the wall, and continued to weep.

I stayed in this place until I felt a release from my spirit. Then, as His peace settled over me again. I pulled myself together and walked back to the front to be with my family. By this time, everyone had gone through the line. Now we gathered around the casket to recall sweet memories, to admire the beautiful flowers that had been sent, or to wait quietly on the front pew until we were ready to leave together.

Public Viewing

At six o'clock, we hosted a public viewing for Bobby at the church where he and others in the family were members. We welcomed friends and acquaintances who had come to say farewell to Bobby and support our family, even at the peak of the COVID-19 pandemic. Although almost everyone was wearing a face mask and standing six feet apart, we were surprised that such a large crowd had shown up.

Under normal circumstances, I don't mind this part of the memorial process. It's an opportunity to reconnect with people you haven't seen in a while and some you've never met. It's a time of sharing, embracing, reminiscing. A time of laughter and tears.

However, with a mask covering the lower half of almost every face, it was difficult to recognize people and much harder to communicate—or even to breathe. I could sense that many were afraid due to so much sickness and death from the virus, so they kept their distance.

Most of my family stood at the front of the church as people lined up to pay their respects. I didn't know many of them, which made it even more difficult. By now, not being accustomed to wearing a mask, I was having a very hard time breathing.

I finally couldn't take it any longer, so I removed the mask. I thought to myself, *This is ridiculous. We are supposed to be Christians. We are supposed to trust God and not be fearful.* If people wanted to keep their distance from me, I had no problem with that. The passing of my brother was difficult enough; I certainly wasn't willing to stand in one place for the next two hours unable to catch my breath!

I said a quick, but silent prayer: *Jesus, protect Your people and help them not to be afraid of the COVID virus. Cover us with Your life-giving blood. I ask this in Your precious name. Amen.*

Finally, around 9:00 P.M. the crowd began to disperse, and we, as a family, were able to say our final goodbyes to Bobby's earthly body. It was during this time that I looked over at the casket and saw my mom standing there with my son, Devin. He had his arm around her shoulders, embracing her as she wept. Before this moment, she hadn't allowed herself to cry in front of anyone. But now she was standing next to Bobby's lifeless body and holding his hand as tears ran down her face. Watching our strong-willed Mama become vulnerable and broken before us brought fresh tears to our eyes.

It was beautiful for me to see my loving, compassionate son comforting his Nanny during this painful moment. As the second grandchild and the first grandson, Devin held a special place in my Mama's heart, and she meant the world to him. A few years later, she shared with me what Devin had said to her that night: *"Nanny, I don't want you ever to go away. Please don't die!"*

"I assured him I wasn't planning to die anytime soon," she told me.

After dropping Samantha, Devin, and the grandkids off at their place, I went to my hotel room and got ready for bed. I was exhausted, thankful for this day to end. Before falling asleep, I whispered a prayer:

"Heavenly Father, thank You for helping me through this difficult day. This trial has taught me how valuable it is to spend time with You, daily, in the secret place. You have prepared me for what I'm going through now. Even though I don't understand why this happened, I am confident You are with me and my family. Thank You for making everything beautiful in its time. Good night, Father."

CHAPTER 10
Seeking His Face

"When You said, 'Seek My face,' my heart said to You,
'Your face, LORD, I will seek.'"

~Psalm 27:8

I set my alarm a little earlier the next morning in order to have extra time with my Beloved. I knew I had to be at the church by 12:30 for the 1:00 P.M. service, and I didn't want to rush my time with Him.

I made myself some coffee and got back in bed, patiently waiting to hear what my Beloved would say to me. It wasn't long before I heard this phrase, *"Seek My face."*

The word *seek* in Hebrew is "to search, look for, inquire about, and make a request." It delights our Beloved King when we seek deeper intimacy with Him. He desires that we search for Him in the "deep-calls-to-deep"' place. It brings Him great joy when we inquire about the situations that come our way. It also brings Him pleasure when we request His help in our decision-making.

He is always available to encourage us in our times of need. He not only wants us to seek Him, He wants us to seek Him *with all our hearts.*

> *"And you will seek Me and find Me, when you search for Me with all your heart."*
> ~Jeremiah 29:13

The Face of God

With that Scripture in mind, I couldn't stop thinking about seeking the face of God. I asked Holy Spirit, "What *is* the face of God? What does it mean to seek His face?"

Holy Spirit reminded me that we are told in Exodus 33:20 that we can't see God's face with the natural eye and live. So, how do we seek His face if we can't see it? We seek His face with the eyes of our spirit.

The word *face* in Hebrew is "appearance, presence, countenance, and favor."

As I continued to think about the face of God, I felt Holy Spirit reveal to me that God's face is His nature. It's His character, His presence, and His favor. His face represents who He is. He then showed me that God has many facets to His face. As we gaze upon Him, He reveals what is necessary according to our particular need. It's like seeing a diamond in the light. When you look at one part, you see something different than if you look at it from another angle.

In Exodus 19, God told Moses that He would make His goodness pass before him. So, God's face represents His goodness, His faithfulness, His love, kindness, longsuffering, peace, mercy, joy, patience, grace, power, holiness, righteousness, justice, truth, etc.

God revealed His goodness to Moses because that's what he needed to move forward on the mission God was calling him to accept. It's the same with you and me. God reveals His nature according to our need. The reflection of His face seems to be the brightest in the times when we need Him most.

"Lord, I trust You to show the reflection of Your face that is needed most today."

The Memorial Service

The memorial service is considered in our American culture as the final day of the memorial process. It is the day we say our earthly goodbyes. However, for the family, it is the beginning of weeks, months and, for some, even *years* of grieving and healing from the passing of their loved one.

I'm reminded that, for those who believe in Jesus, death isn't final. We transition from life on earth to our new life in our heavenly home.

The Scriptures tell us:

"We are confident, yes,
well pleased rather to be absent from the body
and to be present with the Lord."
~2 Corinthians 5:8

It's not that we don't miss those who have gone before us. We do. However, because of Jesus, we can be confident that we will be with them again.

Upon arriving at the church, my family of forty-plus people was directed to one of the Sunday school classrooms. Space was limited, which caused us to feel like sardines in a can! Thankfully, we didn't have to wait very long. Mark came in to offer a prayer, and we all lined up to make our way out to the packed sanctuary.

The memorial service was beautiful. The songs reflected Bobby's true character in Christ. Mark's eloquent words honored him and his life here on earth. He shared funny stories that had everyone in the church chuckling, alternating with tears when he gave testimonies about Bobby and his loving, giving heart.

Once the service was over, we were ushered from our seats to make our way to the gravesite. But I didn't want to leave. I whispered, "Holy Spirit, help me to remain in peace." While sitting in the church, I felt comforted, sensing the nearness of Bobby's earthly body. Taking his body to the burial site seemed so final.

As I exited the church, I broke down, weeping uncontrollably. Once again, the very nature of God, through a familiar verse of Scripture, supported me in my sorrow:

"The LORD is close to the brokenhearted;
He rescues those whose spirits are crushed."
~Psalm 34:18, NLT

After the graveside service, we gathered at Mark's house again for dinner and to spend our final evening with our family. We were exhausted, yet we wanted to be together as much as possible before parting ways.

Knowing I had to travel out of state the next day, I decided to cut the evening short. I said goodbye and hugged everyone before making my way to the car. My drive back to the hotel was quiet. No car radio. No conversation. Not even a prayer. All I wanted was to get back to my hotel room and be still.

When I made it to my room, I put on my PJs, washed my face, brushed my teeth, and crawled into bed. Sitting there, fighting back the tears, I prayed aloud, "Father, I must be honest, I just don't understand why this sudden death. Why now? Why Bobby? He was so young. I'm doing my best to have faith and trust You, yet I'm experiencing emotions I didn't expect. My heart is aching. I'm sad. I'm disappointed. I'm frustrated and angry! This just doesn't seem fair!"

With my heart overflowing and tears running down my cheeks, I cried out, "Lord, I need You! I need You! I need Your help!"

Although I didn't hear a word in response, I felt my Heavenly Father embrace me with His comfort and love as I cried myself to sleep.

Dealing with Grief

The next morning, I was feeling deep sadness. *This isn't like me.* I thought. *"Lord, I can't hear Your voice, and I'm struggling. I can't seem to press past these waves of emotion. I still feel angry, and my heart hurts. I don't know how to deal with this. I'm usually the strong one. It's been a long time since I've had to go through a loss of this magnitude. I know in my heart I must trust You, but I feel stuck. Jesus, even though I can't feel Your presence, I know You are with me. Help me to allow myself to process the grief that's necessary to bring healing to my heart and soul."*

To move forward after any loss, we must experience grief. You never know when it's going to come or how long it's going to last. One minute, you feel okay and it seems you're ready to move forward. Then, out of nowhere, it's as if you are hit by a huge tidal wave of emotions that knocks you off your feet. When you feel a wave coming, allow yourself to experience whatever emotion strikes you and ride the wave until it lifts.

Grief is healthy if you learn how to steer it. Pay attention. If you feel stuck or buried in your thoughts for long periods of time, that's not grief. When you keep replaying something in your mind, that is usually the enemy of your soul. He will cause you to hang onto the thought until you sink into a place of sadness, hopelessness, and at times, even depression. Ask Holy Spirit to help you discern if it's grief or your own thoughts. If it's your thoughts, pull yourself out of the pit of despair and pray.

Moving Forward

Before driving Devin to Wilmington, North Carolina, we spent a little time with Samantha and the girls. Then we stopped by to check on my mom.

On the drive, Devin and I were silent. I was still having a hard time dealing with my emotions, so not talking seemed best at the time. At least, I thought it was. I could tell Devin was struggling to process Bobby's sudden death, too. I asked him if he wanted to talk about it, but he replied, "No, not now." He had never experienced the loss of someone so near to him before, so I knew he would have to process it in his way and in his time.

When we arrived in Wilmington, it was almost nighttime, and I had another five-hour drive to South Carolina, where I would finish my time with my Beloved. With the long drive ahead, it would be best to get a hotel room and leave in the morning. After driving Devin to his place, we prayed together and hugged each other goodbye.

As I drove off, I began to cry. It was difficult leaving him, not knowing when I would see him again or how all of this would affect him. I whispered a short prayer, *"Father, watch over my son. Surround him with angels to protect him. Help him to lean on You for guidance and strength to get through this. Thank You, Father."*

While preparing for bed, I realized that the day had ended, and I hadn't spent any personal time with my Beloved. For the past twenty-nine days, I had gotten up early to give Him the first fruits of my day. However, today I had allowed myself to be so overwhelmed that I had forgotten all about our time together.

I lay face down across the bed and began to cry. I felt so distant from my Beloved King. As I lay there, feeling like I had failed, I heard Him whisper to my heart: *"Peggy, I'm still with you. I've been with you all day, I'm with you every day. Just because you don't feel My Presence, it doesn't mean I'm not with you. I'm with you even when you don't feel Me. I want you to know it's okay if you forget to spend time with Me. You haven't failed Me. I know you are struggling. You don't have to do anything for Me to love you. Just lean on Me and trust Me. I'll get you through this. You are My Beloved Bride, and I love you."*

His words brought so much comfort and reassurance to my grieving heart. I could feel myself being strengthened.

Rejoice!

Just as I was getting ready to turn off the lights and get some sleep, I heard the words of a couple of familiar Scriptures:

> *"Rejoice in the Lord always.*
> *Again I will say, rejoice!"*
> ~Philippians 4:4

> *"Rejoice always."*
> ~1 Thessalonians 5:16

That's it! That's the key! REJOICE! Even when I don't feel like it, I have to push through and rejoice anyway. To *rejoice* is "to be glad, to be delighted, and to have joy." Like me, you are probably wondering, "How can you rejoice when you just lost your brother?" That's a good question.

If I look at the passing of my brother as final, then, yes, it is hard to rejoice. However, if I think of his passing from heaven's perspective, through the eyes of faith, I'll see that my brother is more alive now than he ever was! This gives me the faith to believe that we will be together again when my earthly departure comes. I know that rejoicing is going to take time and effort, but I'm willing to lean on my Beloved to help me walk through the process. Even when I don't feel like it.

One lesson I have learned is that when trials and difficulties come, they can cause our thoughts and emotions to pull us off track. This can give the enemy of our souls an open door to attack us. Therefore, we must stay close to Jesus to avoid falling into the trap of hopelessness and despair.

The Glory of the Lord

On Day 30 of the 40 days with my Beloved, I woke up feeling so much better. Yes, I still missed Bobby, but after the revelation from the night before, I had gained a different perspective. *I'm at peace and choose to rejoice as I trust what I can't see or understand. When the waves of grief hit me, I will ride the waves until they lift, and then I'll move on.*

Before my five-hour drive back to South Carolina, I decided to take a walk on the beach. It was very cold with the January wind blowing across my face, so I bundled up in a heavy coat, scarf, and gloves. The sun was shining brightly, which brought a little warmth. As I increased my pace, I glanced around, thinking, *It is so peaceful here that if I had only brought a blanket, this sandy beach would have been my abiding place for the day.*

As I was finishing my walk, I stood with my feet planted in the sand and allowed the sun to shine on my face for several minutes. I looked out over the ocean once more. The sun was almost blinding as it glistened over the rippling waves. It was as if diamonds were sparkling as far as the eye could see. I could have stood there for hours enjoying God's magnificent creation. Then out of nowhere, I heard the word *GLORY!* This was the word I was to meditate on while driving back.

> *"For the earth will be filled with the knowledge of the Glory of the LORD as the waters cover the sea"*
> ~Habakkuk 2:14

The word *glory* means "splendor, magnificence, grandeur, beauty, respect, honor, and dignity."

On my drive back to South Carolina, I began to think about that verse, especially the phrase, *"the knowledge of the glory of the LORD."* The word *knowledge* in Hebrew is *yada*, which means "to know, to recognize, to understand, to be known, to make oneself known, to be respected, and to have sexual relations or intimacy."

To see the earth filled with the knowledge of God's glory (His "splendor, magnificence, grandeur, beauty, respect, honor, and dignity") as the waters cover the sea is hard to comprehend.

I am filled with excitement and joy knowing that this is a prophecy in God's Word that hasn't been completely fulfilled ... yet. Who knows? We may be the generation to see the fulfillment! We have something wonderful to rejoice over and to look forward to!

I couldn't help thinking of Bobby, knowing he is now with Jesus in all His splendor and glory. He is seeing the angels and all of heaven's magnificence and beauty. This gives me great comfort.

As I continued to ponder this word, I was reminded of the Scripture given to me right before Bobby's passing—John 11:4:

> *"This sickness is not unto death, but for the glory of God, that the Son of God may be glorified through it."*

I asked the Lord, "Why are You bringing this verse to me again? I have accepted the fact that Bobby is gone and am moving forward, knowing that he is in heaven with You."

Then I remembered that I had asked Him why He had given me that verse of Scripture in the first place. So, I waited to hear His response.

He brought to my remembrance Psalm 116:15:

"Precious in the sight of the Lord is the death of His saints."

The Hebrew word for *precious* means "valuable, quality, beloved or splendid, costly, excellent, and honorable."

When connecting the two verses, I could see the big picture. It is *precious* ("valuable, costly, excellent, honorable") in God's sight when one of His children leaves this earthly life to come back Home to be with Him. It brings Him *glory* and it *glorifies* ("gives praise, honor, makes glorious, and magnifies") our King, Jesus.

Now it's making sense. Let's read a passage in the Psalms for more understanding of God's plan for us even before we were born:

"You formed my innermost being, shaping my delicate inside and my intricate outside, and wove them all together in my mother's womb.

"I thank You, God, for making me so mysteriously complex!

Everything You do is marvelously breathtaking.
It simply amazes me to think about it!
How thoroughly You know me, Lord!

You even formed every bone in my body when
You created me in the secret place;
carefully, skillfully You shaped me from
nothing to something.

You saw who You created me to be before I
became me! Before I'd ever seen the light of day,
the number of days You planned for me were
already recorded in Your book."
~Psalm 139:13-16, TPT

I believe, according to these Scriptures, that we were alive with God as spiritual beings in heaven before we were conceived, given a body, and brought here to be born on earth. We were given a specific time in history to come to earth to fulfill God's purpose for our lives. We were even given a certain number of days to live here.

As God's sons and daughters, it is a beautiful, precious thing when we finish our purpose here in this life and go back Home to spend eternity with Him. I believe heaven isn't the same without us, and our heavenly Father longs to see us again. That's why it is so precious to Him when we come Home.

Throughout the remainder of my trip back, I rejoiced with my Beloved as I meditated on the Scriptures He had given me. I'm filled with hope, knowing that when I'm no longer alive in my body, I'll be present with my Lord. I arrived back in Due West, South Carolina, around 4:00 P.M. It felt so good to be back in my hidden place, tucked away in the woods. I unpacked my car, showered, prepared dinner, and climbed into the recliner. I spent the rest of the evening there—resting, unwinding, and reflecting on my journey the past thirty days.

Sacrifice of Praise

Throughout the evening, I rejoiced with my Beloved. I offered Him words of praise and adoration for Who He is—a worthy, mighty King, Lord, and Savior. I thanked Him for comforting and covering me and my family during our painful trial. I thanked Him for the revelation of His Word that had given me a new perspective on eternal life after we leave this temporary earthly life.

Scripture tells us:

> *"Therefore by Him let us continually offer the sacrifice of praise to God, that is, the fruit of our lips, giving thanks to His name."*
> ~Hebrews 13:15

A sacrifice is an act of offering something valuable to God, something that costs us. When we offer a sacrifice of praise, we choose to push past our negative feelings in order to praise Him despite our circumstances. When we do this, the fruit of our words turns His heart toward us to move in our behalf.

I was looking forward to the next ten days with my Beloved. Because of my obedience to come on the journey with Him, I was sure that He had more surprises in store for me as we continued our adventure.

I wanted to say to my Beloved King, *"Thank You for helping me navigate the maze of these last thirty days. It has been a wonderful journey but also challenging. In the beginning, I struggled quite a bit, but I'm so grateful You didn't give up on me. You patiently guided me and gently corrected me when I needed it. I know You have something greater waiting for me. I look forward to seeing how all of this will unfold in the days and weeks ahead. Good night, my Beloved. I love You."*

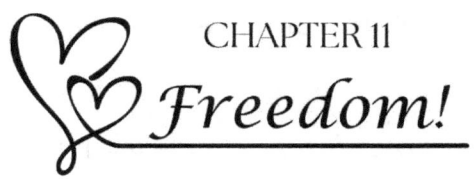

CHAPTER 11

Freedom!

"It is for freedom that Christ has set us free.
Stand firm, then, and do not let yourselves
be burdened again by a yoke of slavery."

~Galatians 5:1, NIV

In this final chapter, I will share a few more insights I gleaned on my quest for more of God, testimonies of experiences, and what I like to call "God Kisses" I received from my Beloved during the last ten days of my journey. You will also learn about my next steps after the journey. It is my prayer that your faith will be built, you will be reminded that nothing is impossible with God, and all things are possible to those who believe.

Freedom in February

On the first day of February, I felt different. The only word to describe it is *freedom*. Freedom in my mind. Freedom in my soul. And my spirit was soaring. I'd been given a whole new perspective on my life in Christ.

I declared this to be the month of moving forward in my newfound life and freedom with Jesus. *"Freedom in February!"*

> *"Therefore, if the Son makes you free,*
> *you shall be free indeed."*
> ~John 8:36

On my morning walk to reflect on the past thirty days, I realized how quickly time had flown by. It seemed like I had just arrived, and now I only had ten days left. *Lord,* I thought, *what is our plan for the remainder of this journey? I want these last few days to be as special as the previous ones. If it's not too much to ask, I'd love to spend a few days at Prayer Mountain.*

I didn't get a response right away, but I know He heard me. He knows this is a desire of my heart.

As an intercessor, I love it when I get the opportunity to take a trip to Prayer Mountain. For those who aren't familiar with this place, it is a mountain located in Moravian Falls, North Carolina, that's been dedicated to the Lord, set apart specifically for prayer. People from all over the world come here to experience God. It's like an open heaven where you can see, hear, and feel His presence in a greater way. Over the years, there have been countless reports of angelic visitations and other supernatural encounters. But for most, it's simply a special place to pray and meditate in silence with only the voices of nature to be heard.

While finishing my walk, I noticed tiny rocks in the pavement glistening in the sunlight. At that moment, my heart whispered, *Jesus, thank You for reminding me how special our walks have been. I feel like Your special Queen who has had You all to herself, and that won't change. However, I desire to take what I have learned on this journey and share it with others. I want to help them encounter You in deeper intimacy and teach them the things you have taught me. I ask for Your wisdom and guidance on how to align with Your plans as we move forward.*

Testimony of God's Goodness

I continued to pray about going to Prayer Mountain. I had been there many times on day trips but had never stayed overnight—a desire of my heart for a long time. With only seven days left before this journey would end, I decided to contact the Apple Hill Lodge to check on prices and see if they had any rooms available. I felt drawn to stay at this lodge because I had visited it in the past and had felt the sweetness of God's presence there. Yes! They had plenty of rooms … all of which were out of my price range!

I decide to go for a walk in the woods to pray. While I was considering ways to make this work financially, I heard my Beloved whisper, *"Just wait."*

I don't have a lot of time to wait, I thought. But I obeyed His request. If this were a test of faith, and it was His plan for me to go, He would provide what was needed.

Shortly afterward, I was invited to visit with some friends who live in the area. During our conversation, I shared with them about my journey and my desire to go to Prayer Mountain. They asked if they could pray for me, and I quickly agreed. I'm always open to receiving prayer.

After we finished, they both told me that the Lord wanted them to bless me financially. My eyes filled with tears. I had not mentioned to either of them that I did not have the finances to stay there. However, my Beloved knew. He spoke to both of my friends individually, and when they came together to discuss it, they shared what Holy Spirit had revealed to them, which was the exact amount I needed for a four-day stay—$500!

What an amazing, faithful King He is.

> *"But seek first the kingdom of God and his righteousness, and all these things shall be added to you."*
> ~Matthew 6:33

His Blessings are Limitless

This is my last day with my Beloved in this intimate resting place, the guesthouse owned by my spiritual family and friends, Dennis and Marge Stoll. Their love and generosity, along with all the Stoll families in this community, have been a tremendous blessing to me on this journey. A blessing greater than I could have imagined. I am forever grateful and will always cherish this hidden place tucked away in the woods.

While preparing to start my day, one of my bridesmaid/intercessors reached out to check on me after my return from my brother's memorial service. I shared with her about the amazing blessing I had received the previous evening.

She began to weep with joy at the thought of God's goodness in providing for me and told me she knew in her heart that I was supposed to go to Moravian Falls. She paused before speaking with even more conviction, "And I believe you are to stay five days instead of four since the number 5 represents God's grace." To prove her point, she sent me another $100 so that I could be blessed with an additional day! *Praise You, Jesus! Thank You for Your faithfulness to guide and provide.*

As my day was winding down, I began to feel the presence of my Beloved drawing me to come sit with Him. I made my way to the recliner to posture my heart and wait on Him. The sweet fragrance of His love swept over my heart like a gentle breeze. As I felt His stirring, tears filled my eyes and flowed down my cheeks. All I wanted was to stay near His heart. I didn't need music or lyrics. All I needed was the tender reminder from His heart that I am His and He is mine.

I say to You, my Beloved King:

"Awake, O north wind! Awake, O south wind!
Breathe on my garden with your Spirit-Wind.
Stir up the sweet spice of your life within me.
Spare nothing as you make me your fruitful
garden. Hold nothing back until I release your
fragrance. Come walk with me as you
walked with Adam in your paradise garden.
Come taste the fruits of your life in me."
~Song of Songs 4:16, TPT

What a beautiful moment as we ended our last night together in this place. As always, when we lay aside our agenda for His, He never disappoints.

Off to Prayer Mountain

The next day, I headed north to Prayer Mountain. I couldn't wait to see what amazing adventures my Beloved had in store for me there.

"Thank You, Father, for this opportunity to join
You on this sacred journey. Thank You, my
Beloved King Jesus, for lavishing me with the
fragrance of Your love in the moments when I
needed it most. Thank You, sweet Holy
Spirit, for being so gentle and kind as You
comforted me, encouraged me, and directed my

140

steps. I'm forever grateful for the time I've been given to be taught by You. It's a journey I'll never forget. Protect me as I drive to my next adventure with You. I love You, Lord, with all my heart!"

I heard my Beloved say: *"Everything is about waiting and timing!"* Upon hearing these words, I wasn't sure what He meant by them. However, over the next several days, He began to speak messages that slowly unfolded His plan for me after the forty days. It was my responsibility to pay attention and journal. And, true to our Creator God, He used a clever, creative method of revealing that plan—"God Kisses."

God Kisses

I arrived at the lodge around lunchtime, feeling like a bride on her honeymoon. The weather was cold and cloudy, but I didn't mind. I was looking forward to visiting my special place at the top of the mountain.

After checking in, since I was the only guest in this three-story lodge, I was given the first choice of rooms. I unpacked my bags and then left to hike up the mountain. The view from the top was breathtaking, even though there were no leaves on the trees. Yet, there is something empowering about being in the *"high place."*

First God Kiss

When I arrived at the summit of the mountain, a lady on the deck was dancing to worship music. She was twirling an eagle flag and a lion flag. It was a beautiful display of adoration of our King.

As I journaled my thoughts about what I was seeing, another lady, who introduced herself as Joy, approached me with a small painting. As best I could tell, it was a painting of a soaring eagle with the face of a roaring lion. The colors were beautiful: turquoise, navy blue, royal blue, yellow, and white—all my favorite colors.

I flipped it over to see what was written on the back: *"Search for me and you will find me! My love for you never ends!"*

I began to cry as I thanked her. She had no idea who I was or the journey I'd been on. She was just being obedient to the Lord. Before she walked off, she said, "He has given you great vision, and He is going to fulfill it!" I wept. The last few days, the Lord had been speaking to me about clarity of vision, but she didn't know this. Her words were confirmation of what He had already been speaking to me.

What a wonderful kiss from my Beloved. I sat there gazing at the painting as I worshipped my King. Part of the picture showed the head of a lion with its mouth wide open as if releasing a roar. I heard my Beloved say, *"When you come out, you will **Soar** and **Roar**!"*

Before leaving to return to the lodge, I sent a picture of the painting to one of my bridesmaids. She told me that she saw what looked like a bride with wings, soaring to greater heights and releasing a sound of great authority.

She said, "Transform, beautiful bride, spread your wings and fly! Your King is carrying you!"

Another Kiss from my Beloved

I made my way back to the lodge. To my surprise, Joy, the lady I met on the mountain had left me another painting. When I walked in the door, there it lay on the table. A beautiful 12x16 canvas painting with an envelope addressed to me.

Inside the envelope was a handwritten note. In the top left corner and the bottom right corner, Joy had drawn a butterfly.

Tears filled my eyes as I read the note. The Lord says, *"For you who are seeking, I am here. You are my beautiful child. Unlike Eve, you have chosen the Tree of Life— life in Me, your Father, your Bridegroom, your God!"*

On the back of the painting was written these words: "Each of the colors in the painting has a special meaning."

Purple—*"I surround you with my royalty."*
White—*"My Spirit is within you."*
Red—*"I shed My blood for you because I love you."*

Green—*"You are full of Life."*
Yellow—*"I fill you with My hope."*

He then said, *"Be the Esther! Be Deborah! Be the Beauty and Love I created you to be! Great Vision, I give. I will provide. Walk with Me. I won't leave you! I love you!*

"Lord, I am overwhelmed by your passionate love for me. Thank you for these two amazing God Kisses."

Third Kiss from my Beloved

As I shared in a previous chapter, God is always speaking. It is up to us to pay attention and listen to how and when. For example, while at the grocery store, I selected some sweet potatoes to purchase. Without realizing it, the last one I picked up was shaped just like a heart. I was blown away. In all my life, I'd never seen anything like this before! Once again, this was a small reminder of His love for me.

Fourth Kiss from my Beloved

Earlier in the day, I was thinking, *Lord, I know snow isn't in the forecast, but it would be wonderful if it snowed during my stay at Prayer Mountain.* A few hours after dinner, I went downstairs to partake of communion and spend some time with my Beloved before midnight. When I walked outside to get some wood to build a fire, to my surprise, it was beginning to snow! My heart leapt! This is a reminder that He hears what we are thinking and answers those prayers as well. *Thank You, Jesus, for another kiss from you.*

"Delight yourself also in the Lord,
and he shall give you the desires of your heart."
~Psalm 37:4

Fifth Kiss from my Beloved

Once the wood ignited and the fire was burning well, I sat back in the recliner to listen to some music and drifted off to sleep. Suddenly, I was awakened at midnight by a bright light. I couldn't open my eyes because of the intensity. It only lasted for a few seconds and then disappeared. I knew it couldn't be from the lamps because the bulbs barely put out any light at all. I had heard about angelic encounters experienced by others in this lodge and felt I had just been visited by an angel myself. All of this, and it's only my first day in this place!

A Blanket of Snow

The next morning, I woke up to a blanket of snow covering the ground of the rolling hills. The view was magnificent. The stillness in the air was so peaceful that I didn't want to move. A pure white snowfall always reminds me of what the prophet Isaiah wrote: *"Though your sins are like scarlet, they shall be as white as snow"* (1:18).

After breakfast, I bundled up to hike up the snowy mountain. Again, the view from the top was spectacular. I sat quietly, listening to birds chirping, an occasional car driving down a distant road, and even the faraway sound of a rooster crowing. Such tranquility. Had it not been so cold, I would have stayed all day.

While preparing to walk back to the lodge, I heard my Beloved say, *"This trip is My gift to you for your obedience and choosing to say YES to Me."*

To hear those encouraging words brought joy to my heart and a smile to my face. The beauty in our obedience is that no matter how difficult it may seem, when we surrender our will to His, we bring delight to His heart. This opens the door for Him to lavish us with His love.

Later in the day, the sun began to peek through the clouds. I sat on the deck all bundled up in a blanket with the wind blowing across my face, watching the sun glistening on the newly fallen snow. Immediately, I was taken back to a simpler time when I was a little girl staying with my grandparents who lived in the country. They lived down a long dirt road. No noise except for the sounds of nature. Only peace. I didn't understand or care about peace back then, but as an adult, I've grown to love and embrace the times when all I can hear is stillness.

We can't always find the time or place to get away for long periods of solitude and quietness. But God's Word teaches us the value of having inner peace and rest in our hearts, minds, and souls as we daily trust Him. These are like hidden treasures waiting to be found.

Once they are discovered, there's no turning back to what once was.

Ask for Angels

During my morning walk, I was thinking about my encounter a few nights before with the bright light. By faith, I believe it was an angel. Throughout the Scriptures, people were visited by angels. Hebrews 1:14 says, *"Are not all the angels ministering spirits sent out (by God) to serve (accompany, protect) those who will inherit salvation? (Of course they are!)"* (AMP).

It occurred to me that I should ask Jesus if He would allow me to see an angel. *"Lord, I've felt angels before, but I've never seen one. Since this is a place with much angelic activity, I thought I would ask You about having my own visitation by sight."*

I then heard Him say, *"Ask for an upgrade of angels in your life!"*

What? Did I hear Him correctly? Then I realized, if He asked me to ask for an upgrade of angels, there is a reason. Is it possible I'm going to need them? I believe I am.

So, with a loud voice, I proclaimed, "YES! YES! Lord, I ask for an upgrade of angels in my life. I call them to come forth in Jesus' name to protect and assist me when I need them!" I could feel the power of Holy Spirit flow through me as I declared these words.

"For He will command His angels in regard
to you, to protect and defend and guard you in
all your ways."
~Psalm 91:11, AMP

We all need protection and assistance. That is part of the angels' assignment from God. If this is a subject you're not familiar with or unsure about, search the Scriptures for yourself. We don't worship angels, and they don't replace our relationship with God, Jesus, and Holy Spirit. However, they have been given the task by God to help us. And I don't know about you, but I can use all the help I can get!

Connecting with Father God

While waiting for my Beloved to meet me that morning, I sensed that something had changed. I feel the love and authority of the Father. I am to honor, connect, and communicate with Him. Most of this journey had been a Bride/Bridegroom connection with Jesus. That was the direction I was led to take at the beginning. However, today feels different. Because I was alone on the mountaintop at the moment, I prayed aloud to my heavenly Father:

"Father, I honor You as my heavenly Daddy. You are so gentle and kind. You are faithful to help me when I'm in need. You always provide for me, comfort me when I am scared, and believe in me when I don't believe in myself. Thank You for being patient with me and for taking

148

great care of me as Your daughter. You lead me in the direction I should go and lovingly correct me when I don't listen. I could go on and on with words to express how I feel about You, but I will end by saying thank You for Your amazing, wonderful love for me. My heart is full and overwhelmed by Your goodness.

Father, today I ask You to help me regain the child in me. I want to learn how to have fun again and not be so serious. I ask You to restore to me my **childlike wonder!** *I love You."*

> *"Who is like You, O LORD, among the gods?*
> *Who is like You, majestic in holiness,*
> *awesome in glorious deeds, doing wonders?"*
> ~Exodus 15:11

What an amazing, wonderful day I had connecting with my loving heavenly Daddy. The weather was bright and sunny with the temperature in the low 60s, which is abnormally warm for the North Carolina mountains in February. We sat on the deck for a while and read the Bible together. Then we went on an exhilarating hike to enjoy the beauty of His creation. What a beautiful gift to spend time with Him.

Our heavenly Daddy knows each of His children as a loving Father should. He knows what touches our hearts and how to bless us in just the simple things of life. I am an outdoor, nature girl, and He knows that about me. I believe

He changed the weather forecast just for me! He desires to shower His children with good things.

What is the desire of your heart today? Talk to your heavenly Daddy about it and trust Him to give you that desire as you delight in Him.

Last Day of the Journey

It is my last day with my Beloved on this journey. I don't want it to end. It has been the most rewarding, life-giving adventure I've ever experienced. How do I go back into the world after being hidden away for forty days? I decided to spend my last day pressing into the heart of my Beloved. I knew He had already paved the way for me and would give me the answers I needed.

I then heard Him say: *"The journey doesn't end here. It is just beginning!* **Tread lightly!***"*

"Thank You, Jesus, for speaking these words of wisdom to me. And now, I want to write You a letter."

Letter to my Beloved

Dear Jesus,

I have so much I want to say to You. How do I begin to thank You? As I sit here pondering my time spent with You on this amazing journey, my heart is overwhelmed with joy, and tears are streaming down my face. Thank You for leading, prompting, encouraging, and comforting me with patience and kindness.

My Beloved King, You have captured my heart like no other. I will forever cherish what I have discovered in this sweet time we've had together. You have taken me to a whole new level of intimacy as You've showered me with Your love, provision, and kisses from Your life-giving Word.

Lord, You brought healing to my heart and soul. You've given me greater confidence in who I am and my identity in You. With Your help, I'm ready to go back into the world and help others discover this beautiful journey with You, whatever that looks like for each individual.

As I transition back into the world, help me not to get caught up in the busyness of life and neglect what has been cultivated in this beautiful season of my life with You.

I love You, my King, with all my heart!

Peggy

So now, with the wind of Holy Spirit beneath my wings, I will Soar from this place like the mighty, majestic Eagle and Roar with the Lion of the Tribe of Judah!

Here we go! Let's do this!

Acknowledgments

Writing a book is not for the faint of heart. It takes motivation and dedication. It also takes a tribe of people who believe in you and are dedicated to helping you cross the finish line. These are those I would like to acknowledge.

First, I want to honor my editor, Anne Severance. Over the past two-plus years, Anne has not only been my editor, prayer partner, and encourager, but she has also become my dear friend and spiritual mama. I asked God for the best editor, and He sent the best to me. I love you, Anne, with all my heart, and I am forever grateful that God chose you for me.

Next, I want to honor a man of integrity and excellence, Todd Engel. God chose Todd as the gifted designer of this book cover, and from the beginning, it has been perfect. Thank you, Todd, for creating God's masterpiece.

To my incredible Prayer Shield: Debbie Cella, Jeanine Siebold, Sara Kleppinger, Nancy Horning, Paulina Elor, and Rita Williams, who is celebrating from heaven. I am forever grateful for your prayer covering for me and all that pertains to this book. You are my heroes, and I love all of you.

To my dearest friends, Cindy Edwards, Danielle LaFaye, Stacey Langston, and Allison Rolston, thank you for your faithful sisterhood, prayers, and encouragement throughout the years I've known you.

To my writing coach, Missy Worton, and the tribe of Warrior Writers, thank you for your insight, coaching, and encouragement.

To the Stoll Families from South Carolina, for your hospitality and generosity in blessing me with a place to stay during my journey. You are my second family.

To those who blessed this book financially, thank you for your generosity and for your obedience to the voice of God. I honor you.

Last but certainly not least, I want to thank my daughter, Samantha, for her understanding when I wasn't available during countless hours of writing. Thank you for believing in me. I love you.

♡About the Author

Since her salvation in April 1989, Peggy Adams has been a lover of God's Word. Her love of His Word has driven her hunger to know Jesus personally, not just to know about Him. Peggy is an author, ordained minister, speaker, and prophetic intercessor. She is the founder of KingdomVoice-418, a ministry established by God according to Luke 4:18 to bring freedom to those in spiritual bondage.

Peggy graduated from New Day Apostolic School of Ministry in Colfax, North Carolina, in May 2015. From there, she was called by God to move to Nashville, Tennessee, where she served with many local leaders as a prayer missionary. She was the Prayer Director of the Nashville House of Prayer and helped mobilize prayer throughout the greater Nashville area as well as for other national events. She helped lead the History Makers prayer conference call for nine years. Peggy was ordained as a minister through B-Mosaic, an Apostolic Leadership Alliance, in September 2019.

Peggy's greatest desire is to teach and encourage the Bride of Christ to know her identity in Him. From her own personal journey of intimacy with Jesus, the Lord has instructed her to help lead and teach others to discover a deeper, more intimate relationship with Him.

When she isn't serving in ministry, her favorite pasttimes are hiking, spending time in the mountains, and sitting on the beach reading. Peggy is the mother of two children: her daughter, Samantha, and her son, Devin, who is in heaven, and her two granddaughters, Avah and Ariyah.

After her own forty-day journey of being hidden away with Jesus, He asked her to help teach others how to go on their own personal daily journey through an invitation with Him on a "30-Day Journey in the Secret Place." If you are interested in more information about this or for speaking engagements, please contact her at pjadams50@gmail.com or on FB Messenger.

www.kingdomvoice418.com

www.ingramcontent.com/pod-product-compliance
Lightning Source LLC
Chambersburg PA
CBHW061757120626
46550CB00005B/2035